Eliot Attridge, Trevor Baker, Adam Bay
Dorothy Warren and Steve Wisema

ESSENTIALS
OCR GCSE
Science A

Contents

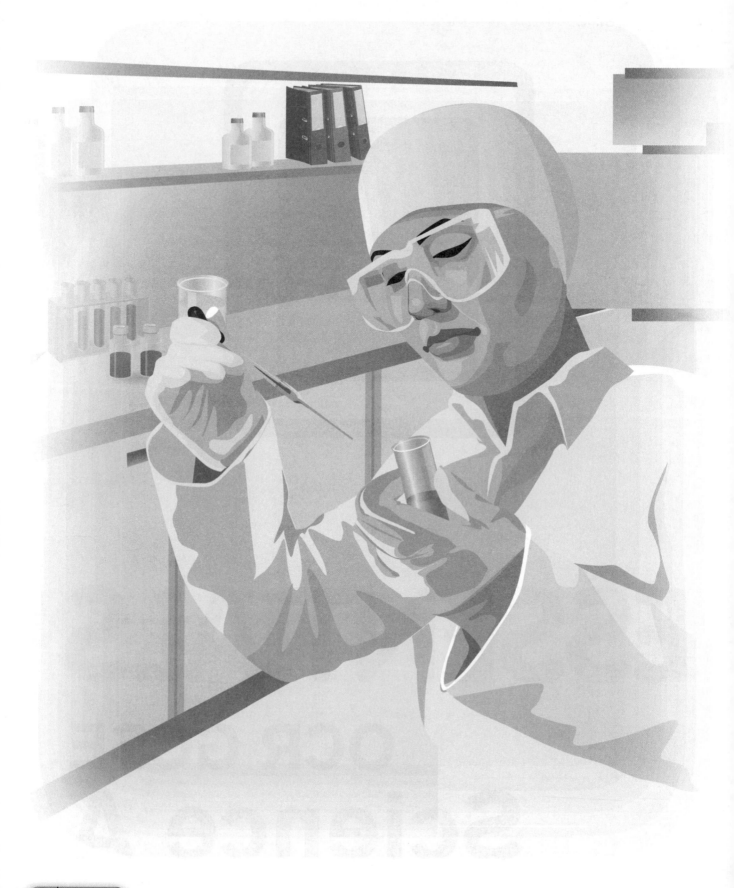

Contents

1. Read the following newspaper article.

Little Sleep for Mexican Blind Cave Fish

In April, 2011, biologists reported in the journal, *Cell*, that Mexican Blind Cave Fish had evolved the capacity to cope with less sleep than the surface variety of the fish. They had observed that surface fish clearly slept at night, having been found inactive at the bottom of the laboratory tank with their fins drooping. The variants that were found in caves, however, patrolled the laboratory tanks all night. The temperature of the water in the tanks was kept constant.

The researchers allowed the two variants to breed and studied the behaviour of their offspring.

	% Sleeping at Night	% Awake at Night
Surface fish	100	0
Cave fish	0	100
Hybrid offspring	40	60

(a) Which of the following is **not** a possible hypothesis for the experiment? Put a tick (✓) in the box next to the correct answer. [1]

There will be a difference in the offspring due to pH. ☒

There will be a difference in the offspring due to the water temperature. ☐

There will be a difference in the offspring due to the air quality. ✓

There will be a difference in the offspring due to the amount of light. ☐

(b) The researchers were sure that their evidence showed that the trait for coping with a lack of sleep was inherited. What evidence did they have to show this? [1]

60% of offspring stayed awake at night

(c) If 250 offspring were born during the experiment, calculate how many offspring would be awake at night. Show your working. [2]

250 ÷ 100 x 60 = 150

(d) The researchers used 12 of each type of fish. What could you say to criticise this experiment and, consequently, how could you improve it? [1]

they didn't use enough fish therefore its less accurate

(e) The researchers hypothesised that the cave fish did not necessarily need less sleep. Instead they believed the cave fish needed to stay awake more to allow them to catch more food, which in a cave may be scarce. What aspect of Ideas about Science does this represent? Put a tick (✓) in the box next to the **best** answer. [1]

Thinking creatively ✓   Thinking scientifically ☒

Thinking quickly ☐   Thinking abstractly ☐

2. Spinal Muscular Atrophy (SMA) is a **recessive** disease that causes the nerve cells of sufferers to degenerate.

   (a) If the symbol for the recessive allele is **a**, what will the alleles be in a person who does **not** carry the disorder? [1]

   AA

   (b) Look at the family tree below showing the inheritance of SMA in a family.

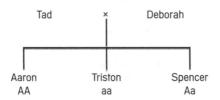

   What alleles are carried by...

   Tad? Ac   Deborah? Aa   [1]

   (c) Spencer married Alev. Alev has no family history of SMA. They want to have children. Explain the chances of them having a child with the disorder. Why is it useful to be able to test adults for the presence of harmful alleles and what are the risks?

   ✏ *The quality of written communication will be assessed in your answer to this question.* [6]

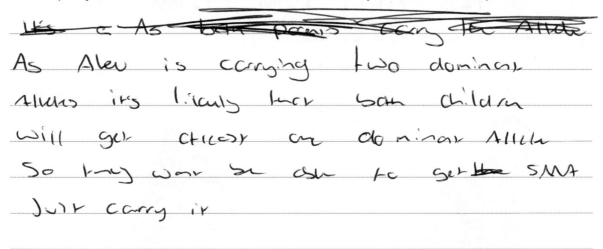

   As Alev is carrying two dominant alleles its likely that both children will get chlcosy an dominan Allele So they wont be able to get the SMA Just carry it

3. Genetic diseases, such as Huntington's disease and cystic fibrosis, have symptoms. Draw straight lines from each of the genetic diseases to their symptoms. [4]

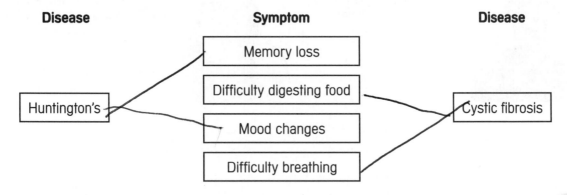

4. **(a)** Read the following article about predictive testing for genetic diseases.

> ## Is Predictive Testing the Answer?
>
> **1** There are many genetic disorders that afflict people around the world.
>
> **2** It is now possible to test adults, children and embryos to see if they carry a faulty allele.
>
> **3** In the case of embryo testing, there are two genetic tests: chorionic villus sampling and amniocentesis.
>
> **4** With both of these tests, there is a chance that having the test will cause the premature death of the embryo.
>
> **5** Each year, 1 in 200 amniocentesis tests ends in the miscarriage of the pregnancy.
>
> **6** Some people argue that we should not end the lives of unborn children in this way; others argue that it prevents suffering in the future.

(i) Which **two** sentences contain a statement about risk? Write the numbers of the sentences. [1]

 4 , 5

(ii) Which sentence, **1**, **2**, **3**, **4**, **5** or **6**, gives a statistic about risk? [1]

 5

(b) Which of the following measures of risk is the highest? Put a ring around the correct answer. [1]

1 in 20   （1 in 5）   1 in 100   1 in 1000   2 in 40

5. Some friends are discussing 'designer babies'.

Samuel
Altering DNA is unnatural. It is against God.

Damiie
I'd only like to have male babies.

Darby
There are certain times when altering the DNA of a zygote is necessary – when trying to prevent the passing on of a dangerous genetic disorder, for example.

Gwyneth
The Government has to regulate designer babies on a case by case basis using evidence, not just emotion. The decision will take account of what's right and what's wrong.

(a) Who has made a statement which gives a scientific reason for allowing designer babies? [1]

Darby

(b) Who has made a statement which indicates that ethics have to be considered? [1]

Gwyneth

6. A study suggests that shoe size increases with a student's intelligence between the ages of 4 and 16.

(a) Why would it be wrong to try to increase a student's shoe size in an attempt to improve their intelligence? Put ticks (✓) in the boxes next to the **two** correct statements. [2]

Adult shoes have extra tax on them. It is better to keep to smaller shoes to save money. ☐

Although there is a correlation, it does not necessarily mean that there is also a cause. ☑

As children grow, their feet grow too. In addition, as they grow their brains will develop more. ☑

It's the other way round: improving intelligence leads to bigger feet. ☐

(b) In a class of students, the range of shoe sizes is from size 1 to size 12. On the axes below draw the line graph that you would expect to get if the shoe sizes were measured and plotted. Label the *y*-axis. [2]

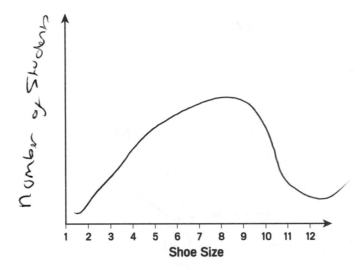

7. In 2010 in the UK, identical quads went to school for the first time.

(a) Which statement explains how identical quads are formed? Put a tick (✓) in the box next to the correct statement. [1]

One egg was fertilised by four sperm. ☒

Two eggs were both fertilised by a sperm and then they both separated. ☐

One egg was fertilised by one sperm which then divided and separated once. ☐

One egg was fertilised by one sperm which divided once and then separated, and then each cell divided and separated again. ☑

(b) The quads will share certain features. Which statement will definitely be correct throughout the quads' lives? Put a tick (✓) in the box next to the correct statement. [1]

They will have the same fingerprints. ☐

The way their ear lobes are attached will be the same. ☑

They will have the same allergies. ☐

They will like the same music. ☐

(c) The chance of giving birth to identical quads is given as 1 in 64 000 000. Explain what the **1 in 64 000 000** statement means. [2]

that our of 64,000,000 births 1 will

be identical quads

(d) Although the quads look the same, their parents can recognise them. Why is this so? Put a tick (✓) in the box next to the **best** statement. [1]

The quads have different names. ☐

The environment causes subtle differences. ☑

Some genes are always different. ☐

Their fingerprints are different. ☐

[Total: _____ / 32]

Higher Tier

8. Monosodium Glutamate (MSG) is a chemical flavouring often added to Asian foods, such as Chinese and Japanese meals. It adds the umami flavour to food. It is caused by the body tasting the molecule glutamate, which is found naturally in tomatoes, mushrooms and broccoli.

A small number of people are not able to taste the chemical. This is due to a taste receptor, known as TASR1, being faulty.

The gene that codes for the TASR1 receptor responsible for MSG recognition is given as M.

(a) State the **genotype** for a heterozygous individual. [1]

Mm

(b) State the **phenotype** of a person with mm alleles. [1]

Car tasn MSG

(c) If someone is a carrier for the allele and has children with another carrier, what is the chance of having a baby who is…

(i) a carrier? [1]

50%

(ii) homozygous recessive and so unable to taste MSG? [1]

25%

(iii) completely free of the condition? [1]

50% x 25%

(d) If someone is a carrier for the allele and has children with another carrier, what would the ratio of…

(i) the genotypes be? [1]

MM , Mm, mm

(ii) the phenotypes be? [1]

3:1

9. Adele was 16 when she discovered that she did not carry the sex-determining region Y (SRY) gene. She had assumed that the fact that she had never had a period had been due to having polycystic ovaries, which her sister has. However, after seeing her doctor and having a genetic test, she discovered that she did not carry the SRY gene.

Which statements about Adele's condition are scientifically correct? Put ticks (✓) in the boxes next to the **two** correct statements. [2]

Adele has the body type of a female, including uterus, fallopian tubes, cervix and vagina. ☐

Adele has the sex chromosomes XXY. ☐

Adele has the sex chromosomes XY. ✓

Adele's body cannot detect the hormone androgen. ✓

10. Explain the procedure for pre-implantation genetic diagnosis (PGD). Suggest what the ethical issues are with this technique.

✎ *The quality of written communication will be assessed in your answer to this question.* [6]

once fertilised the embryos split into 8 cells. then a single cell is selected from the womb and tested for the genetic disorder. If positive the parents may choose to kill the embryos. However this will lead to loss abortion and many believe that it is unnatural

11. Embryonic stem cells are seen as having the potential to cure many genetic diseases. Which statements best describe embryonic stem cells? Put ticks (✓) in the boxes next to the **three best** statements. [2]

Embryonic stem cells...

...can be taken up to the 40th day of pregnancy. ☐

...can only be taken from an embryo up to the 8 cell stage. ✓

...can be harvested from any part of the body. ☐

...have the potential to become any cell type. ✓

...are unspecialised cells. ✓

12. A group of students is discussing whether the Government should force people to have genetic tests.

April
Having a genetic test will help to target illnesses earlier. It can only help to save lives.

Jonathan
But genetic testing would mean that you may not get insured! If you carry a gene for coronary heart disease, it doesn't mean that you will get it.

Matthew
If the information fell into the wrong hands it could be terrible.

Skirmante
You could be tested to check if a drug is likely to work on you. That could prevent suffering.

(a) Which **two** students are suggesting benefits of genetic testing? [1]

_____April_____ and _____Skirmante_____

(b) Which **two** students are suggesting negative consequences? [1]

_____Matthew_____ and _____Jonathan_____

13. Read this newspaper article.

Testing for Intolerance

At some stage in our lives we may need to take medicinal drugs. The problem is that drugs are developed and tested on relatively small numbers of individuals.

Unfortunately, some of us may suffer side effects, for example some painkillers can cause stomach ulcers.

Sometimes drugs will not even work as the patient does not have the correct receptor for the drug to work.

The advent of genetic testing promises to usher in an era of personalised medicine. Patients will be able to take only those drugs that will work for them and have minimal side effects.

(a) Explain what is meant by **personalised medicine** and why knowing what genetic variants are carried is so important for deciding what drugs a patient is given. [3]

because everyone has a different set of genes not all medicin will work on everybody. by personalising medicine you look at the persons genes and create a treatment which will work for them

(b) Genetic tests can have a variety of outcomes. Considering these, give two potential problems that can arise when using genetic testing to see if you are likely to suffer from side effects and either benefit or not benefit from a drug. [2]

the drug could damage your organs
If your result is a false positive you could receive drugs that may harm you just like a false negative

(c) The Government could make it the law that you **have** to have your genome screened and stored on a genetic database. It would then be a simple process to determine whether a drug is suitable or not. Give one argument why this may not be a good idea. [1]

Information could be seen by the wrong people, employers may no longer want to employ you

14. Read the newspaper article.

From Frogs to Dolly

Dolly the sheep was the first mammal to be cloned from adult body cells. Before Dolly, scientists had been trying to obtain clones from other animals. It was very difficult: how could you prove that the new organism was a clone?

In 1952, frogs were cloned by scientists. They took green frogs and extracted their eggs. The DNA was removed and DNA from albino frog tadpoles was introduced. When the frogs grew up, they were all albino.

In 1997, an egg from a black-faced ewe was taken and the DNA from the mammary gland of a Finn Dorset ewe was introduced. After electrical stimulation the egg started to divide and form an embryo.

Eventually, one of the eggs successfully grew into the sheep known as Dolly. However, out of 217 embryos, Dolly was the only one that successfully grew into an adult sheep. She died six years later.

(a) Suggest why using animals with very different looks from the donor of the egg are used. [1]

....

(b) Calculate the percentage efficiency of the technique that led to Dolly. Show your working. [2]

....

(c) Unlike cloning mammals such as Dolly the sheep, cloning humans is banned by international law. Some people, however, would argue that we should be able to allow cloning. Discuss the arguments for and against cloning humans.

✏ *The quality of written communication will be assessed in your answer to this question.* [6]

....

....

....

....

....

....

(d) To date it has only been possible to clone frogs, unlike mammals such as Dolly, from embryonic cells. What conclusion can be made? Put a tick (✓) in the box next to the **best** answer. [1]

Frogs are more advanced organisms. ◯

DNA degenerates over time. ◯

Not all genomes of adult cells can lead to the development of a new organism. ◯

It is a complete mystery which scientists will never solve. ◯

[Total: .... / 35]

1. This question is about the immune system.

   (a) Which statement about the immune system below is **incorrect**? Put a tick (✓) in the box next to the answer. [1]

      Some white blood cells hunt for microorganisms in the body. ☐

      Microorganisms have antibodies on their surface. ☑

      White blood cells can engulf microorganisms. ☐

      Memory cells use antibodies to detect and kill the microorganism. ☑

   (b) A scientist has announced to the press that he has discovered a new cell in the immune system. He has not yet published his results. Which is the **best** reason why other scientists may be sceptical about his statement? Put a tick (✓) in the box next to the best answer. [1]

      The scientist is not necessarily an expert in his field. ☐

      He is only in it for the fame. ☐

      Other scientists have not been able to check his results. ☑

      The immune system is already completely understood. ☐

2. A new bleach says that it kills '99.99% of bacteria'.

   (a) If there were 1 000 000 bacteria in your toilet, how many would be left immediately after treating it with the bleach? Show your working. [2]

   (b) The doubling time of the bacteria in the toilet is 30 minutes. What is the maximum number of bacteria after cleaning the toilet and then leaving it for 5 hours? Show your working. [2]

   (c) Give **three** conditions that aerobic bacteria need to survive. [3]

     1.

     2.

     3.

3. In 2010, a scientific study carried out by the Food Standards Agency showed that 65.2% of all chickens sold in supermarkets was contaminated with *Campylobacter* – the cause of the majority of food-poisoning cases in the UK.

Cooking chicken thoroughly and washing areas that have come into contact with the raw meat kills *Campylobacter*. Each year, 400 000 people get food poisoning from *Campylobacter* and 80 people die. *Campylobacter* can be treated with antibiotics.

(a) Assuming that the UK population is 61 000 000, calculate the following. Show your working.

(i) The percentage of the population that gets food poisoning from *Campylobacter*. [2]

(ii) The percentage of the population that dies from *Campylobacter* food poisoning. [2]

(iii) Why is it important to know the difference between these figures? [1]

(b) Why would it be wrong to say that chickens cause 400 000 people to get *Campylobacter* food poisoning each year? Put ticks (✓) in the boxes next to the **two best** answers. [2]

There is a correlation, which means there is a cause. ⬭

There is a correlation, which only suggests that there may be a cause. ⬭

There are other sources of *Campylobacter*. ⬭

Campylobacter is a virus and can be found everywhere. ⬭

(c) Astra is worried by the study. She believes that the risk is so great that she will not eat meat any more. Many people make decisions in similar ways every day. Explain why her decision not to eat meat is not necessarily a good idea and why people make mistakes understanding risk.

🖊 *The quality of written communication will be assessed in your answer to this question.* [6]

4. MMR is a vaccine that protects against three dangerous diseases: mumps, measles and rubella (German measles). Some friends are discussing vaccination.

Siobhan
I am not going to chance giving my daughter the MMR vaccine. She may get autism. Although there's a risk of getting the diseases, it's not worth it.

Salma
Everyone else is vaccinated. There's no need for me to get my children vaccinated.

Spencer
My grandad lost his twin sister at the age of 12 and he became blind, all because they caught measles.

Ian
No-one has measles nowadays. There's no point having the vaccine.

(a) Three of the friends have underestimated the risk that can occur from not having the vaccine. Who has **not** made this mistake? [1]

_____

(b) Who is confusing the small risk of a side effect with the much larger risk of catching the disease? [1]

_____

(c) Who is relying on a large enough pool of vaccinated people to keep the disease at bay? [1]

_____

(d) Some people argue that vaccination is not worth the risk. Explain how vaccination works and suggest what problems may happen when too few people are vaccinated.

🖊 *The quality of written communication will be assessed in your answer to this question.* [6]

5. Complete the following sentences. Use words from this list. [4]

liquids   **bacteria**   **viruses**   **chemicals**   **kill**   **grow**

Antimicrobials are _____ that _____ bacteria, fungi and viruses.

Antibiotics are a type of antimicrobial which are only effective against _____. They

are not effective against _____, which is why you are not given them when you

have flu.

6. Tuberculosis (TB) is a disease caused by a bacterium. Read the newspaper article and then answer the questions that follow.

TB – Could it Return?

A The vaccine BCG, which protects against the killer disease tuberculosis (TB), ceased to be given routinely to children in the UK in 2005.

B BCG was 80% effective against the bacterium that causes TB.

C Having the vaccine resulted in a painful blister on the arm that eventually formed a permanent scar.

D Now the BCG vaccine is only given to infants who are living in regions where the rate of TB is greater than 40 cases in 100 000 people or to infants who are in close contact with the disease. These infants are at a higher risk.

E Although TB is relatively rare in the UK, it is more common in parts of Eastern Europe.

F This is partly due to sufferers not completing the course of antibiotics when they are diagnosed with the disease. The antibiotics have to be taken over a period of six months.

G Some people want to have the BCG vaccine, regardless of its efficacy to protect against the disease.

H Doctors say that if too many people have the disease, then the BCG vaccine will be ineffective. This is because new strains will emerge.

(a) (i) Which **two** paragraphs give reasons why the vaccine BCG is **not** given to all children in the UK now? Write the letters of the two paragraphs. [1]

_____ and _____

(ii) Which paragraph, **A, B, C, D, E, F, G** or **H**, gives the reasons why certain children still receive the vaccine in parts of the UK? [1]

_____

(iii) Which paragraph, **A, B, C, D, E, F, G** or **H**, explains why it is believed that TB is more common in Eastern Europe? [1]

_____

(iv) If the population of London is 8 000 000 and the rate of TB cases is 40 in 100 000, how many people could be expected to have TB? Show your working. [2]

_____

_____

_____

(b) Why will new strains of TB emerge if too many people catch the disease? [1]

_____

_____

(c) On the axes provided, draw the graph that you would expect to see if a patient with TB **completed** their course of antibiotics. The dashed line on the graph represents the number of harmful bacteria in the body at the start of the treatment. [1]

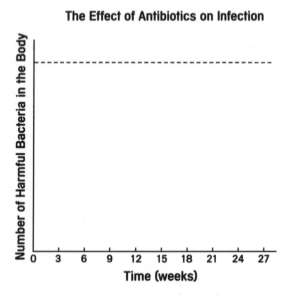

7. **(a)** What is the **ethical** reason why doctors may not give a placebo to a patient as part of a medical trial? [1]

_____

_____

(b) When might it be difficult to hide whether a patient was on a placebo or not? [1]

....

....

8. Brian is suffering from coronary heart disease. Nobody in his family has died of a heart attack in the past.

(a) What are the most likely reasons for Brian's disease? Put ticks (✓) in the boxes next to the **two** best statements. [2]

He regularly gets stressed at work. ☐ He is vegetarian. ☐

He must carry the genes for heart disease. ☐ He regularly smokes. ☐

(b) Zara is another patient at the same clinic that Brian attends. There have been a large number of patients with heart disease from the part of the country where Zara lives.

What type of study should doctors carry out to find out the cause? Put a ring around the correct answer. [1]

epidural   ecclesiastical   academic   epidemiological

9. To keep reptiles, such as a bearded dragon, a special habitat has to be set up for them to live in. This is called a vivarium. The diagram shows a vivarium.

Heat lamp ☐

Thermometer ☐

Thermostat ☐

(a) (i) Write **R** in the box next to the part of the vivarium which is a **receptor**. [1]

(ii) Write **E** in the box next to the part of the vivarium which is an **effector**. [1]

(iii) Write **P** in the box next to the part of the vivarium which is a **processor**. [1]

(b) Explain what is meant by **homeostasis**. [1]

_____

_____

(c) If a mammal was placed in the vivarium, instead of a lizard, what external input would no longer need to be controlled? [1]

_____

(d) Which of the following statements best describes homeostasis in lizards? Put a tick (✓) in the box next to the best statement. [1]

It is impossible for lizards to control their body temperature. ◻

Lizards are cold-blooded. ◻

Lizards have to use the environment to keep their bodies warm. ◻

Lizards are mammals. ◻

10. (a) The amount of water that has to be reabsorbed in the body depends on a number of factors. For each of the factors below, decide if a high amount of the factor will lead to concentrated or dilute urine and put ticks (✓) in the correct boxes. The first one has been done for you. [4]

Factor	Urine is concentrated	Urine is dilute
High amount of fluid drunk	◻	✓
High amount of exercise done	◻	◻
High external temperature	◻	◻
High amount of alcohol drunk	◻	◻
High amount of the drug Ecstasy taken	◻	◻

(b) Where in the body is water reabsorbed from the blood? [1]

_____

11. Look at the charts for each patient, then answer the questions that follow.

Kathy	**Birendra**	**Jason**	**Mary**
Female	Male	Male	Female
Age 48	Age 50	Age 19	Age 39
Height 165cm	Height 180cm	Height 177cm	Height 158cm
BMI 24	BMI 36	BMI 16	BMI 29
Blood pressure 119/70	Blood pressure 149/90	Blood pressure 100/50	Blood pressure 135/89

(a) What are the risks of each person having a heart attack? Explain your reasons.

✎ *The quality of written communication will be assessed in your answer to this question.* [6]

....

....

....

....

....

....

....

....

....

(b) What symptoms might Jason be suffering from? Assuming he is not suffering from a disease, what advice would you give to Jason? [3]

....

....

....

....

(c) What piece of equipment is used for measuring blood pressure? [1]

....

[Total: .... / 68]

Higher Tier

12. Bacteria grow exponentially. An equation that can be used for the calculation of exponential growth is shown below.

$$x = a \times 2^n$$

This equation enables biologists to calculate the number of bacteria (x) after the population has doubled a given number of times. a = the number of bacteria at the start; n = the number of times the population has doubled.

(a) There are five spores of *Listeria monocytogenes*, a bacterium that causes the deadly disease listeriosis, on a supermarket sandwich. Assuming all the spores start to grow at the same time with a doubling time of 20 minutes, what will the **maximum** number of bacteria be after 24 hours? Show your working. [3]

(b) In practice, numbers of bacteria such as the one you calculated in part (a) will never be reached. Suggest why. [2]

13. Read the following report and then answer the questions.

TeGenero was a company that specialised in creating new drugs. TBN1412 was a drug that was intended to help patients suffering from B-Cell Leukaemia (a disease where memory cells are prevented from making antibodies).

The testing of TBN1412 followed government guidelines. The drug, which was expected to do its job well, had been tested on animals before being tested on humans. For the first human trial, eight male volunteers were involved. Two of the volunteers were given a placebo and the other six were given a dose of TBN1412 that was 500 times lower than that given to the animals. Neither the trial males nor the doctors administering TBN1412 knew whether the trial males were receiving a placebo or the drug itself.

After 5 minutes, six of the eight men started complaining of headaches and pain. Shortly after that, the men started reporting that they felt like they were on fire. All six of the males who received the drug had to be admitted to intensive care.

The drug caused a 'cytokine storm', which is a potentially fatal immune reaction. Cytokines are released by white blood cells to attract other cells to destroy the invader. Unfortunately, with TBN1412 a cytokine storm was triggered and cells started attacking all parts of the immune system. The reaction was completely unanticipated. None of the animals that were tested had any adverse reaction.

The drug trial was reported in the media as being a failure and referred to as a 'drug trial gone wrong'.

(a) What is the name of the type of trial the eight men were involved in? [1]

....

(b) The British press had headlines stating that the trial was a failure. Explain why the trial was seen as having failed and suggest reasons why it could be regarded as having succeeded.

🖉 *The quality of written communication will be assessed in your answer to this question.* [6]

....

....

....

....

....

....

....

....

....

(c) It is now thought that the reason why TBN1412 did not show adverse effects in the animals tested was because the drug targeted memory cells and the animals, unusually, did not have any memory cells when they should have had them. The animals that had been tested were monkeys, which have the same immune system as humans. They were only different to wild monkeys in that they were bred and raised in laboratory conditions.

What is the most likely reason why the monkeys did not have memory cells? Put a tick (✓) in the box next to the correct answer. [1]

The monkeys had been genetically engineered, so they did not have memory cells. ◯

Monkeys are not related to us, so do not have the same immune system. ◯

As they were raised in sterile conditions, the monkeys had not been exposed to disease. ◯

The monkeys' memory cells must have come into contact with TBN1412 in the past. ◯

(d) The monkeys' dose had to be scaled down for the humans. If the dose given to the monkeys was 1.2mg, what would the dose in the human volunteers have been? [2]

14. The table shows how the body loses water. An adult loses 3000cm³ of water in one day.

(a) Complete the table to show the volume of water lost through each method. [4]

How Water is Lost	Percentage	Volume of Water Lost Each Day (cm³)
Urine	40	
Faeces	5	
Sweat	45	
Breathing	10	

(b) (i) What is the name of the hormone that controls the concentration of urine? [1]

(ii) What happens to the production of this hormone when alcohol is consumed? [1]

(iii) What happens to the production of this hormone when the drug Ecstasy is consumed? [1]

[Total: _____ / 22]

1. Zebras and donkeys are members of different species. Zebras can mate with donkeys to produce offspring called zonkeys.

   (a) Which of the following Venn diagrams **best** illustrates the relationship between zebras, donkeys and zonkeys? Put a tick (✓) in the box next to the best diagram. [1]

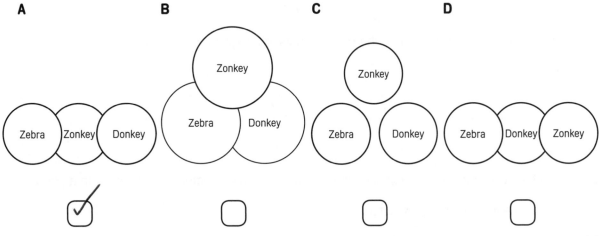

A   B   C   D

   (b) What is the definition of a **species**? [1]

   _____

   _____

2. The diagram shows a food web.

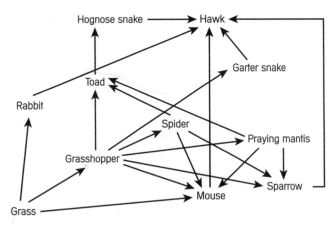

   A disease has reduced the mouse population to very low numbers.

   (a) What feeds on praying mantises? [1]

 toad, sparrow, ma

(b) Predict what will happen to the grasshopper population. Explain your answer. [1]

....

....

....

(c) Predict what will happen to the rabbit population. Explain your answer. [1]

....

....

....

3. The following information describes the feeding relationship between organisms in a pond.

Water beetles eat mayfly nymphs.

Mayfly nymphs feed on algae.

Water beetles are eaten by sticklebacks.

(a) Draw a **food chain** to illustrate this information. [2]

(b) Which organism is the **autotroph** in this food chain? [1]

....

(c) Which herbivore is a **heterotroph** in this food chain? [1]

....

(d) How many trophic levels are in this food chain? [1]

....

(e) Give **two** ways in which energy is **lost** from this food chain. [2]

1. ....

2. ....

(f) What type of organism breaks down other organisms after they die? [1]

....

4. **(a)** The diagram shows the carbon cycle. Name the processes **1** to **6** by completing the key below. [4]

1. ....

2. ....

3. ....

4. ....

5. ....

6. ....

(b) Why is life on Earth said to be carbon-based? [1]

....

5. The number of fish in the River Lonsdale has been decreasing. Scientists have been called in to find out why.

(a) The scientists first measure nitrate levels using a dip stick. These are the results:

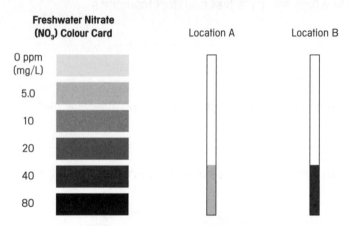

How much nitrate is present at each of the locations tested? [1]

Location A: _____ ppm   Location B: _____ ppm

(b) The following organisms were found at location A: mayfly nymph, trout, stonefly nymphs.

The following organisms were found at location B: bloodworms, rat-tailed maggots.

Explain why the organisms are different at the two locations and suggest why using living organisms is useful.

🖉 *The quality of written communication will be assessed in your answer to this question.* [6]

....

....

....

....

....

....

....

6. **(a)** Scientists study how long ago life started on the Earth and how it evolved. Put a ring around the correct options in these sentences. [3]

Life is thought to have evolved **2500 / 3500 / 4500** million years ago. One piece of evidence

for this is from **radiological dating / the Bible / eye witness testimony**. There is evidence that

fewer / the same number of / many other species previously existed compared with today.

(b) A group of students is discussing evolution.

Becky
All life on Earth shares a common ancestor. You just need to look at the fossil record and the shared genes that organisms have.

Naveen
Evolution by natural selection is a fact.

Christine
Life on Earth came from a comet that landed on the Earth.

Alan
God put all animals and plants on the Earth. It is clearly written in the Bible.

(i) Who is making a religious argument? [1]

_____

(ii) Who is referring to scientific evidence? [1]

_____

7. In 2010, scientists discovered fossil remains that they believed were a new cousin of modern humans, nicknamed 'Denisovians'. They are thought to have cross-bred with humans. Other scientists were not so sure. They thought that the skeletal remains were just a type of Neanderthal.

Which of the following **best** describes why scientists could reach a different conclusion given the same evidence? Put a tick (✓) in the box next to the best answer. [1]

Scientists have travelled back in time to see the original species. ◯

There is not enough evidence to reach a firm conclusion. ◯

Scientists always stick to what they believe. ◯

It is more fun when there is controversy. ◯

8. In 1999, the British Government passed a law intended to prevent products being sold with excess packaging. In 2010, the law was used to take a large supermarket to court, as it was selling fresh beef with too much packaging.

(a) Packaging is a problem because it ends up being thrown away. Where does the packaging typically end up? [1]

(b) Even if the packaging is biodegradable, it is still a problem as it decomposes slowly when there is not enough oxygen. Suggest why the packaging decomposes slowly at a landfill site compared with elsewhere. [1]

(c) What **three** things do manufacturers have to consider when designing packaging that will have a minimal effect on the environment? [3]

1.

2.

3.

(d) The case against the supermarket was the first of its kind in the UK. Packaging costs the supermarket money. Suggest one reason why the supermarket sold the beef with excess packaging, assuming that the contents were adequately protected. [1]

(e) What does the term **sustainability** mean? [1]

9. The diagram shows the energy flow through a food chain.

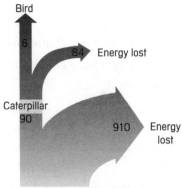

(a) Calculate the percentage of the energy successfully transferred to the caterpillar feeding on the plant. Show your working. [2]

(b) Explain where the energy goes at each stage and suggest why scientists are interested in understanding this.

✎ The quality of written communication will be assessed in your answer to this question. [6]

[Total: .... / 46]

10. At Whitley Wood in the New Forest, biologists discovered that a British species of earthworm was being outcompeted by an invading species which is common in southern Europe. The table below shows data gathered from the wood.

No. of British Earthworms in 1990	100 per m³
No. of British Earthworms in 2010	10 per m³

The biologists say that this **proves** that global warming is affecting the climate in the UK. Other scientists disagree. They argue that the data is not reliable enough. Why do they say it is not reliable? Put a tick (✓) in the box next to the **best** answer. [1]

The biologists should not have used earthworms; humans would have been better. ◯

The biologists did not use a satellite to track the temperature changes. ◯

The biologists did not record the colour of the earthworms. ◯

The biologists did not look at other similar locations in the UK to see if the worms were affected in the same way. ◯

11. Biological material will decay over time. There are a variety of organisms that carry out decay. Draw straight lines to show whether each organism is a decomposer or a detritivore. [2]

Organism	Type
Earthworm	
	Decomposer
Bacteria	
Woodlouse	
	Detritivore
Fungus	

12. Nitrogen is a vital element for survival. Even though 79% of the atmosphere is nitrogen gas, animals cannot use any of it.

(a) State the **two** ways that nitrogen is fixed into a form useable by animals and plants. [2]

1. _____

2. _____

(b) The diagram shows the nitrogen cycle.

Write the correct number, **1**, **2**, **3** or **4**, in each box. [3]

Eaten by animals ◯

Denitrifying bacteria ◯

Nitrifying bacteria ◯

Nitrogen-fixing bacteria ◯

13. Give the names of **three** processes, other than reproduction, that, when combined, can lead to the formation of a new species. [3]

1. ....

2. ....

3. ....

14. Read the newspaper article.

Evolution Proved?

In 1988, Richard Lenski started a simple experiment that many now believe has proved evolution.

Lenski set up 12 identical flasks containing the bacterium *Escherichia coli* (*E. coli*) and, every day, 1% of the contents of each flask was subcultured into new flasks of fresh growth media.

Every 500 generations Lenski preserved samples from each population. He stored the samples on agar plates and put them in cold storage. This was equivalent to being a fossil record of the experiment.

In 2010, the 50 000 generation milestone was reached.

After approximately 33 000 generations, bacteria in one flask were suddenly able to consume citrate, a molecule that *E. coli* had never previously been able to use as an energy source.

(a) Why is storing samples every 500 generations like creating a fossil record? [1]

....

....

(b) In what ways is this process **not** like the fossil record? [2]

....

....

(c) What must have happened to the DNA of the *E. coli* in the flask where they were able to utilise citrate as an energy source? [1]

....

(d) Some anti-evolutionists argue that evolution is really just selective breeding. Explain what selective breeding is and argue why this is **not** the case with Lenski's experiment and why his experiment is evidence for evolution.

🖉 *The quality of written communication will be assessed in your answer to this question.* [6]

....

....

....

....

....

....

....

....

(e) What could a scientist do to prove whether or not the citrate-consuming *E. coli* were the result of a random mutation? Put ticks (✓) in the boxes next to the **two best** statements. [2]

Repeat the experiment.

Go back to an earlier generation and see if the same mutation occurs again.

Use technology to see how the DNA has changed.

Splice the genes and add to a virus vector.

[Total: .... / 23]

1. Fossil fuels, such as natural gas (methane), petrol and diesel, consist of compounds called hydrocarbons.

    (a) Explain what is meant by the term **hydrocarbon**. [1]

        a compound of hydrogen and carbon

    (b) Burning a fossil fuel is an example of a chemical reaction. Which **two** words describe the reaction that takes place when a fossil fuel burns? Put ticks (✓) in the boxes next to the **two** correct answers. [2]

    Respiration ☐

    Combustion ☑

    Reduction ☐

    Oxidation ☑

    (c) Complete the diagram to show what happens when methane burns in pure oxygen. [3]

    Methane   +   Oxygen   ⟶   Carbon dioxide   +   Water

    Key: ● Carbon   ◍ Oxygen   ○ Hydrogen

    (d) Explain what is meant by the term **incomplete combustion**. [1]

    (e) Explain why the car industry is spending millions of pounds developing new technologies that will eventually replace the combustion engine. [4]

2. This question is about the Earth's atmosphere.

The Earth's first atmosphere was formed by volcanic activity. It consisted mainly of water vapour and carbon dioxide but no oxygen.

(a) Use words from the list to complete the sentence and answer the questions about how the early atmosphere changed. A word may be used once, more than once or not at all.

photosynthesis   dissolving   condensed   evaporated

heated   cooled   respiration   combustion

(i) As the Earth _cooled_ , water vapour _condensed_ and the oceans formed.

[1]

(ii) Which **two** processes were involved in the reduction of carbon dioxide levels? [2]

_____

(iii) Which process explains why levels of oxygen started to increase? [1]

_____

(b) Approximately how much oxygen and nitrogen is in the atmosphere today? [1]

Oxygen: _____ Nitrogen: _____

(c) Describe and explain how both human activity and natural causes are changing the composition of today's atmosphere.

✎ _The quality of written communication will be assessed in your answer to this question._ [6]

_____

_____

_____

_____

_____

_____

_____

_____

_____

_____

3. Scientists have found a correlation between the amount of pollen in the air and the incidence of hay fever in people who have a pollen allergy. Initially, scientists looked at thousands of medical records. The graph below shows what they found. Despite these results, this correlation was considered not to be conclusive and further skin tests had to be carried out.

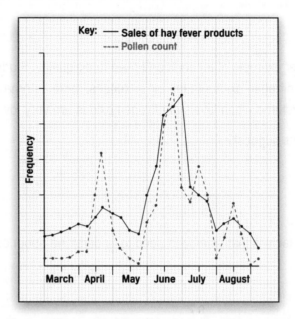

(a) Using the data in the graph, explain what the scientists found and why their results were not considered to be conclusive. [3]

....

....

....

....

....

....

(b) The results from the skin tests are given in the table below.

Skin Test	Hay Fever Sufferers	Non Hay Fever Sufferers
Pollen stuck to skin	Skin became red and inflamed	No visible effect

Explain how these results provide a link between pollen and hay fever. [2]

....

....

....

(c) How would scientists ensure that the evidence collected was reliable, accurate and reproducible?   [2]

....

....

....

(d) Asthma is another example of a condition linked to air quality. Studies have shown that when the concentration of nitrogen oxides in the air increases, more asthma attacks occur. However, people still suffer from asthma when levels of nitrogen oxides are very low.

(i) What does this suggest?   [1]

....

....

(ii) Suggest **two** factors that scientists need to understand about asthma.   [2]

1. ....

2. ....

4.   Air pollution is everywhere and it affects us all. We all have a responsibility to reduce it. The two main sources of air pollution are motor vehicles and power stations that burn fossil fuels.

(a) Which of the following increase car emissions? Put ticks (✓) in the boxes next to the **two** correct answers.   [2]

A fuel-efficient engine ☐   Using low-sulfur fuel ☐

Always driving to the shops ☐   Switching to bio-diesel fuel ☐

Driving a hybrid car ☐   Buying a car with a bigger engine ☐

Using public transport ☐

(b) By fitting a car with a catalytic converter, the amount of carbon monoxide and nitrogen monoxide entering the atmosphere is reduced. Use the word equations to write balanced symbol equations.

(i) Carbon monoxide   + Oxygen   ⟶   Carbon dioxide   [2]

.... + ... ⟶ ....

(ii) Nitrogen monoxide   + Carbon monoxide ⟶ Nitrogen   + Carbon dioxide   [2]

.... + ... ⟶ .... + ...

(c) What can be used to decrease the emissions from a coal-fired power station? Put ticks (✓) in the boxes next to the **two** correct answers. [2]

Fitting a filter system ☐   Using hydroelectricity to power it ☐

Increasing production ☐   Using oil to power it ☐

(d) Following an international meeting about climate change in Kyoto, Japan, in 1997, people from many countries agreed to reduce carbon dioxide emissions. Targets were set for the individual countries, which continue to meet regularly. The governments of the countries are required to take appropriate measures to meet the targets.

(i) Describe what is being done in the UK on a national and local level to meet these targets and explain how new legislation could have an impact on the local economy.

🖉 *The quality of written communication will be assessed in your answer to this question.* [6]

....

....

....

....

....

....

....

....

....

....

(ii) Suggest why governments in different countries may consider taking different actions to try to reduce carbon dioxide emissions. [2]

....

....

....

....

....

(e) Suggest how an individual person could help to reduce air pollution. [2]

....

....

....

....

5. (a) Many of the pollutants found in the atmosphere are a result of human activity. In parts (i) to (iv) below are the names of four pollutants. Use as many of the following key words as possible to describe where they come from.

power stations **fossil fuels** **combustion engine**

burning **incomplete combustion** **coal**

(i) Carbon dioxide: .... [1]

....

(ii) Nitrogen monoxide: .... [1]

....

(iii) Sulfur dioxide: .... [1]

....

(iv) Carbon particulates: .... [1]

....

(b) Complete the table with the formulae of the molecules shown. Use the key to help you. [4]

Name	Formula	Molecule
Carbon dioxide		
Nitrogen monoxide		
Water		
Sulfur dioxide		

Key: ● Carbon   ◉ Oxygen   ○ Hydrogen   ● Nitrogen   ⊗ Sulfur

(c) Atmospheric pollutants cannot just disappear; they have to go somewhere. Draw straight lines to show what happens to each of the pollutants. [4]

Pollutant	What happens to it
Carbon dioxide	Used by plants during photosynthesis
Sulfur dioxide	Deposited on buildings
Carbon particulates	Reacts with water to form acid rain
Nitrogen oxides	

(d) Here is some data about carbon monoxide collected from a city centre:

Carbon monoxide (ppm)	5.3	5.6	5.2	5.9	5.5

(i) Why is the level of carbon monoxide carefully monitored in many city centres? [1]

(ii) It is not possible to give a true value for the concentration of carbon monoxide but it is likely to lie within the range of the collected data. Complete the statement below about the range of the data. [1]

The range is _____ ppm to _____ ppm.

[Total: ____ / 64]

Higher Tier

6. This question is about gases that are found in the atmosphere.

(a) The early atmosphere was formed by volcanic activity. Over millions of years the atmosphere slowly changed. Today's atmosphere is very different. Describe these differences. [2]

(b) The atmosphere began to change when green plants started to grow on Earth. In your own words, explain what you think happened. You will need to include information about how the amount of carbon dioxide and oxygen changed and what caused the changes.   [3]

(c) Suggest reasons why today's atmosphere is constantly monitored by scientists.   [4]

7.   Data are important to scientists because they can be used to test a theory or explanation. Rebecca and Tom collect data to test whether sulfur particulates are an example of a pollutant caused by human activity. They collect the data in the centre of a town and in a country park, on the same day. Their results are shown below.

Time	Concentration of Sulfur Particulates (ppm)	
	Town Centre	Country Park
3.00pm	2.5	0.2
4.00pm	0.3	0.1
5.00pm	3.0	0.1
6.00pm	3.5	0.2

(a) Suggest **three** reasons why it is not possible to find the true value for the concentration of the sulfur particulates. [3]

....

....

....

....

(b) What is the range of values shown in the town centre? [1]

.... ppm to .... ppm

(c) Why is it so important to repeat measurements? [3]

....

....

....

....

(d) Which measurement is the outlier in the data? [1]

.... ppm

(e) Work out the best estimate of the true values for each set of results. Show all your working. [4]

....

....

....

....

....

....

....

....

(f) How do these results relate to the theory that sulfur particulates are an example of a pollutant caused by human activity? [2]

....

....

....

(g) Is there a significant difference between the mean concentrations of sulfur particulates in the town centre and the country park? Give reasons for your answer. [2]

....

....

....

....

8. The Intergovernmental Panel on Climate Change (IPCC) is concerned about emissions of nitrogen oxides from aircraft.

(a) (i) Why are nitrogen oxides produced in the aircraft engines? [2]

....

....

(ii) The reaction takes place in two stages. Complete the equation for stage one. [3]

Nitrogen + Oxygen ⟶ ....

●● + ⊘⊘ ⟶ ☐

(iii) During the second phase of the reaction, which process produces the nitrogen dioxide? Put a tick (✓) in the box next to the correct answer. [1]

Combustion ☐   Displacement ☐

Reduction ☐   Respiration ☐

Oxidation ☐

(b) Explain what is meant by the term **NO$_x$**. [2]

....

....

(c) Suggest why the IPCC is concerned about NO_x emissions from aircraft. [2]

....

....

....

(d) Since the introduction of catalytic converters on new cars, the level of NO_x produced in city centres has dropped. Complete the equation to show what happens in a catalytic converter.

Nitrogen monoxide + Carbon monoxide ⟶ .... + ... [3]

9. Sulfur dioxide is produced as a by-product by many coal-fired power stations. It is often removed from the flue gases by wet scrubbing using an alkaline slurry.

(a) How does sulfur dioxide get into power station flue gases? [2]

....

....

....

(b) Complete the following sentence. Use a word from this list. [1]

        oxidised   **absorbed**   **reduced**

During wet scrubbing, sulfur dioxide is .... by the alkaline slurry.

(c) Why is it necessary to remove the sulfur dioxide? [2]

....

....

[Total: .... / 43]

C2 Material Choices

1. In everyday life we use many different materials. Some are produced from natural resources; others are produced by chemical synthesis.

   (a) The table below shows different types of material.

   Put a tick (✓) in the correct column to show how each material is produced. [4]

Material	Natural Resources	Chemical Synthesis
Nylon		
Wood		
PVC		
Wool		

   (b) The table below shows some of the properties of the materials. Complete the third column by stating a suitable use for each material. [4]

Material	Properties	Uses
Nylon	Lightweight Stretchy Strong Waterproof	
Wood	Quite a good insulator of heat Hard and rigid Waterproof	
PVC	High tensile strength Tough and durable Not very stretchy Waterproof	
Wool	Medium strength Good insulator of heat Stretchy Adsorbs water	

(c) Strength and elasticity are important properties of a climbing rope. Manufacturers test the fibres before they make them into ropes.

Here are the results of a series of tests of the strength of a nylon fibre:

Test Number	1	2	3	4	5
Strength (kN)	616.0	617.5	616.2	615.9	616.8

(i) Suggest reasons why the test was carried out five times. [3]

....

....

....

....

(ii) What is the range of the data shown in the table? [1]

.... kN to .... kN

2. Crude oil is a very useful raw material. It is a thick, black, sticky liquid made up of a mixture of hydrocarbons.

(a) What is the name given to the process of separating crude oil? Put a tick (✓) in the box next to the correct answer. [1]

Fractional crystallisation ▢   Fractional decanting ▢

Fractional distillation ▢   Fractional partition ▢

(b) Name the elements present in a hydrocarbon. [1]

....

(c) Different hydrocarbons have different boiling points because their molecular chains are different lengths. Explain why the separation of crude oil depends on this fact. [3]

....

....

....

....

....

3. Many leading sports-clothing manufacturers now use antibacterial fibres containing silver nanoparticles in their garments to help keep them fresh. Some experts are worried about the possible effects on the skin of long-term exposure to nanoparticles.

(a) A group of students is talking about nanoparticles.

Darby
A nanoparticle is the width of a human hair.

Gwyneth
A nanoparticle is the width of a few atoms.

Jonathan
Nanoparticles have a large surface area compared to their volume.

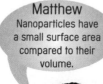

Matthew
Nanoparticles have a small surface area compared to their volume.

Deborah
Nanoparticles are polymers.

Which **two** students are making correct statements?   [2]

.... and ....

(b) Name **two** other products that use nanoparticles and explain how the nanoparticles change the properties of the material used to make the products.

   ✏ *The quality of written communication will be assessed in your answer to this question.*   [6]

....

....

....

....

....

....

(c) Suggest why some experts are worried about the possible effects on the skin of long-term exposure to nanoparticles. [3]

4. A Year 6 class has been asked to design some seats for their playground, so that groups of children can sit down and chat during breaks. The chairs must have these qualities:

- Strong enough to sit on
- Cheap to buy
- Easy to move
- Not dangerous

They have to decide what material to use, so they carry out some tests. Here are the results:

Material	Strength	Density	Cost
Iron	Very strong	High	Medium
Wood	Strong	Medium	High
Polypropene	Strong	Low	Low

After much discussion the majority of the class agreed to choose polypropene.

(a) Suggest why the majority of the class chose polypropene. Use the information in the table to support your answer.

✎ *The quality of written communication will be assessed in your answer to this question.* [6]

(b) Some of the class were not happy with the decision because they thought that polypropene was bad for the environment. Which statements explain why? Put ticks (✓) in the boxes next to the **two** correct answers. [2]

Polypropene is made from a non-renewable material. ◯

Polypropene is grown in hot countries. ◯

Polypropene comes in bright colours. ◯

Polypropene can be recycled. ◯

Polypropene is non-biodegradable. ◯

(c) Two members of the class thought that iron chairs would be better in windy weather. Explain why. [2]

....

....

[Total: .... / 38]

Higher Tier

5. PVC is produced from small molecules by the process of polymerisation. The diagram represents one of these molecules.

● Carbon   ◍ Chlorine   ◯ Hydrogen

(a) What is the chemical formula of the small molecule used to produce PVC? Use the key to help you. [1]

....

(b) What is the name given to small molecules that can join together to form polymers? Put a tick (✓) in the box next to the correct answer. [1]

Polymers ◯   Repeat units ◯

Minimisers ◯   Monomers ◯

(c) Briefly describe what happens during polymerisation. [2]

....

....

OCR Twenty First Century GCSE Science A Workbook Answers

Answering Quality of Written Communication Questions

A number of the questions in your examinations will include an assessment of the quality of your written communication (QWC). These questions are worth a maximum of 6 marks and are indicated by a pencil icon (✎).

Your answers to these questions will be marked according to...
• the level of your understanding of the relevant science
• how well you structure your answer
• the style of your writing, including the quality of your punctuation, grammar and spelling.

QWC questions will be marked using a 'Levels of Response' mark scheme. The examiner will decide whether your answer is in the top level, middle level or bottom level. The expected quality of written communication is different in the three levels and it will always be considered at the same time as looking at the scientific information in your answer:
• To achieve Level 3 (which is the top level and is worth 5–6 marks), your answer should contain relevant science, and be organised and presented in a structured and coherent manner. You should use scientific terms appropriately and your spelling, punctuation and grammar should have very few errors.
• For Level 2 (worth 3–4 marks), there may be more errors in your spelling, punctuation and grammar, and your answer will miss some of the things expected at Level 3.

• For Level 1 (worth 1–2 marks), your answer may be written using simplistic language. You will have included some relevant science, but the quality of your written communication may have limited how well the examiner can understand your answer. This could be due to lots of errors in spelling, punctuation and grammar, misuse of scientific terms or a poor structure.
• An answer given Level 0 may contain insufficient or irrelevant science, and will not be given any marks.

You will be awarded the higher or lower mark within a particular level depending on the quality of the science and the quality of the written communication in your answer.

Even if the quality of your written communication is perfect, the level you are awarded will be limited if you show little understanding of the relevant science, and you will be given Level 0 if you show no relevant scientific understanding at all.

To help you understand the criteria above, three specimen answers are provided to the first QWC question in this workbook. The first is a model answer worth 6 marks, the second answer would be worth 4 marks and the third answer worth 2 marks. The three exemplar answers are differentiated by their scientific content and use of scientific terminology. Model answers worth 6 marks are provided to all other QWC questions to help you aspire to the best possible marks.

Module B1: You and Your Genes (Pages 4–13)

1. **(a)** There will be a difference in the offspring due to the air quality **should be ticked**.
   (b) Any one from: 60% of the offspring stayed awake at night; Only 40% of the offspring slept at night.
   (c) Any one from: 0.6 × 250 = 150 offspring; (60 ÷ 100) × 250 = 150 offspring
   [1 for correct working but wrong answer]
   (d) The sample size was too low. Increasing the sample size would improve the reliability of the experiment.
   (e) Thinking creatively **should be ticked**.

2. **(a)** AA
   (b) Tad: Aa
   Deborah: Aa
   (c) This is a model answer which would score full marks:
   As Spencer is a carrier of the SMA allele, he has the dominant allele A and the recessive allele a. Alev has no family history of SMA, so it is likely that she is carrying both dominant alleles. If they were to have children, each child would get at least one dominant allele, so none of the children would have the condition. Testing adults for genetic disorders means that people have a better idea of the chances of their future offspring getting a disorder. However, the tests are not 100% reliable and could lead to couples choosing not to have children when they actually do not carry the disorder.
   This answer would score 4 marks: None of the children would get it as Alev must be AA. This means that every child would definitely get a dominant gene. As the disease is recessive, there is a 100% chance they would not have the disorder. Testing means that the parents would have a better idea of what genetic disorders their child may have.
   This answer would score 2 marks: Spencer has Aa. One of his children might get the disease because they could get the a gene from him but not from Alev, who does not carry it.

3. **Lines should be drawn from** Huntington's **to** Memory loss **and** Mood changes.
   Lines should be drawn from Cystic fibrosis **to** Difficulty digesting food **and** Difficulty breathing.

4. **(a) (i)** 4 and 5 **[Both needed for 1 mark.]**
       (ii) 5
   (b) 1 in 5 **should be ringed**.

5. **(a)** Darby
   (b) Gwyneth

6. **(a)** Although there is a correlation, it does not necessarily mean that there is also a cause **and** As children grow, their feet grow too. In addition, as they grow their brains will develop more **should be ticked**.
   (b)

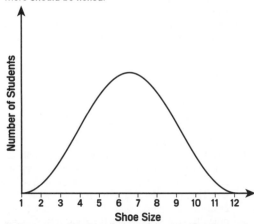

[1 for a correctly shaped curve; 1 for labelling the y-axis **Number of Students / Frequency**. Accept a bar chart which shows a normal distribution curve.]

7. **(a)** One egg was fertilised by one sperm which divided once and then separated, and then each cell divided and separated again **should be ticked**.
    (b) The way their ear lobes are attached will be the same **should be ticked**.
    (c) That in every 64 000 000 successful births **[1]** only one will be of quads **[1]**
    (d) The environment causes subtle differences **should be ticked**.

8. **(a)** Mm
    (b) Cannot taste MSG
    (c) **(i)** **Any one from:** 1 in 2; 0.5; $\frac{1}{2}$; 50%

    (ii) **Any one from:** 1 in 4; 0.25; $\frac{1}{4}$; 25%

    (iii) **Any one from:** 1 in 4; 0.25; $\frac{1}{4}$; 25%

    (d) **(i)** Ratio MM : Mn : mm would be 1 : 2 : 1
    (ii) Ratio able to taste : not able to taste would be 3 : 1

9. Adele has the sex chromosomes XY **and** Adele's body cannot detect the hormone androgen **should be ticked**.

10. **This is a model answer which would score full marks:**
    In vitro fertilisation is undertaken. Each resulting embryo has a single cell removed when it arrives at the 8 cell stage. The single cell is tested to see if the allele for the genetic disorder that is causing concern is present. If it is not, then the embryo is implanted into the mother and the pregnancy continues as normal. If it has the disorder, the embryo is destroyed. The ethical issues are that, rather than allowing a prospective embryo to develop normally, we are choosing which one will have the chance. There is a risk to the embryos that are tested − removing a cell could have an effect in the long term on the development of the child. There is also an argument that the non-implanted embryos should not be destroyed as they too could have developed into a human being.

11. …can only be taken from an embryo up to the 8 cell stage; …have the potential to become any cell type **and** …are unspecialised cells **should be ticked. [2 for all correct; 1 for two correct]**

12. **(a)** April; Skirmante **[Both needed for 1 mark.]**
    (b) Matthew; Jonathan **[Both needed for 1 mark.]**

13. **(a)** Personalised medicine is where the particular genes that a patient has are taken into account when planning their treatment **[1]**. Some drugs may not work with some people and new technology means a drug can be given only to those that it will work on **[1]**. It also means that side effects should be minimised and the chance that the treatment will be successful should be improved **[1]**.
    (b) If the result is a false positive, then you will not receive a drug which may have helped you **[1]**. If the result is a false negative, then you will be prescribed the drug when it will cause side effects **[1]**.
    (c) **Any one from:** Employers may use the information to not employ you; Insurers may not cover you; The information could fall into the wrong hands.

14. **(a)** So that it is possible to tell whether the organism is a clone or not
    (b) 1 in 217 eggs / embryos grew
    Percentage efficiency = 1 ÷ 217 × 100
    = 0.46%
    [1 for correct working but wrong answer]
    (c) **This is a model answer which would score full marks:**
    The process of cloning mammals is very inefficient. The success rate with Dolly the sheep was 0.46%, which is very low. If this was repeated with humans, there would be lots of embryos that would die or fail to develop, and a large proportion of the population is against this. People would also argue that too many eggs need to be collected and these could potentially have become human beings. On the other hand, some scientists may want to clone humans to provide supplies of organs, which could be used to save

lives. There will also be a small number who want to do it as a challenge, to push the boundaries of science.
    (d) Not all genomes of adult cells can lead to the development of a new organism **should be ticked**.

Module B2: Keeping Healthy (Pages 14–24)

1. **(a)** Microorganisms have antibodies on their surface **should be ticked**.
    (b) Other scientists have not been able to check his results **should be ticked**.

2. **(a)** 1 000 000 × 0.9999 = 999 900;
    1 000 000 − 999 900 = 100
    or 1 000 000 × 0.0001 = 100
    [1 for correct working but wrong answer.]
    (b) 5 hours = 5 × 60 minutes = 300 minutes
    $x(t) = a \times b^{t/\tau}$
    $= 100 \times 2^{300/30}$
    $= 100 \times 2^{10}$
    $= 100 \times 1024$
    $= 102\,400$ bacteria
    [1 for correct working but wrong answer]
    (c) **Any three from:** Water; Oxygen; Food; Heat

3. **(a)** **(i)** (400 000 ÷ 61 000 000) × 100 = 0.66%
    [1 for correct working but wrong answer]
    (ii) (80 ÷ 61 000 000) × 100 = 0.00013%
    [1 for correct working but wrong answer]
    (iii) It enables people to work out the chance of getting food poisoning and the chance of dying from *Campylobacter*, so they can make an informed decision about buying chicken.
    (b) There is a correlation, which only suggests that there may be a cause **and** There are other sources of *Campylobacter* **should be ticked**.
    (c) **This is a model answer which would score full marks:**
    Everything we do carries a risk. The risk with *Campylobacter* is relatively small, with less than 1% of people getting this type of food poisoning and a very small number dying from it. Food poisoning does not only come from meat; it also comes from not washing your hands and not cleaning vegetables. The press sometimes over-emphasise risk or make it seem higher than it actually is by only reporting newsworthy stories. If someone has had food poisoning before, they may be more familiar with the risk and fear it more. Not eating meat also carries a risk − we need the protein and vitamins to grow. In future, Astra washing her hands and work surfaces, as well as cooking meat thoroughly, will minimise the risk.

4. **(a)** Spencer
    (b) Siobhan
    (c) Salma
    (d) **This is a model answer which would score full marks:**
    Vaccination involves injecting a safe form of the disease-causing microorganism into the body. White blood cells recognise the antigens on the surface of the vaccine. The white blood cells then 'remember' the antigens, so when the real disease is caught, it is killed before it kills the patient. Diseases which have a vaccine against them are either potentially life-threatening or do considerable harm when caught, for example, causing brain damage or making the patient sterile. The side effects of the vaccine are normally not very serious or are much rarer than getting the disease itself. Therefore, the benefit of having the vaccination outweighs the risk of a side effect. If too few people are vaccinated, then there will be a pool of people that the disease could flourish in, eventually mutating and infecting those who were vaccinated previously.

5. chemicals; kill; bacteria; viruses

6. **(a)** **(i)** **Any two from:** B; C; E **[Both needed for 1 mark.]**
    (ii) D

(iii) F

(iv) 40 cases in 100 000

so 40 × 80 = 3200 cases in 8 000 000

[1 for correct working but wrong answer]

(b) The larger the pool of people with the disease, the greater the chance of a bacterium emerging that has mutated into a new strain.

(c) Any suitable graph which starts at the dashed line and decreases as a curve, ultimately ending at 0 on the *y*-axis, e.g.

The Effect of Antibiotics on Infection

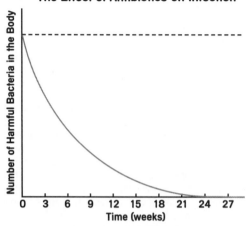

7. **(a)** It is not right to withhold a medical treatment that could cure someone or make them feel better. A placebo has no effect.

(b) When the drug causes an obvious effect.

8. **(a)** He regularly gets stressed at work **and** He regularly smokes **should be ticked.**

(b) epidemiological **should be ringed.**

9. **(a) (i)–(iii)**

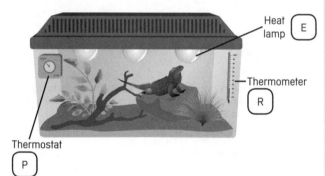

(b) Homeostasis is the maintenance of a constant internal environment.

(c) Temperature

(d) Lizards have to use the environment to keep their bodies warm **should be ticked.**

10. **(a)**

	Urine is concentrated	Urine is dilute
High amount of fluid drunk		✓
High amount of exercise done	✓	
High external temperature	✓	
High amount of alcohol drunk		✓
High amount of the drug Ecstasy taken	✓	

[1 for one correct; 2 for two correct; 3 for three correct; 4 for all four correct]

(b) The kidneys

11. **(a) This is a model answer which would score full marks:**
Birendra is most likely to suffer from a heart attack. This is because his BMI is 36, which is much higher than the highest healthy reading of 25. Birendra's blood pressure is also very high, suggesting there is a lot of pressure in the arteries. High BMI and blood pressure are indicators for a heart attack. Mary is overweight and has an increased chance of having a heart attack. Kathy has a normal BMI, which means her body mass is within the normal range for her height. It is unlikely that she will have a heart attack based on her BMI. Jason's BMI is low. His chance of suffering a heart attack is low, although he may have other health problems.

(b) Jason will probably feel tired and light-headed **[1]**. His BMI suggests that he is underweight **[1]**. He should try to increase the amount of food in his diet **[1]**.

(c) A sphygmomanometer

12. **(a)** $n = (24h × 60min) ÷ 20min$

$n = 72$ **[1]**

$x = a × 2^n$

$x = 5 × 2^{72}$

$x = 2.36 × 10^{22}$ bacteria

[1 for second calculation and 1 for correct answer. Allow error in first step carried forward to second half of calculation.]

(b) After a certain number of generations, food, space and other factors become limiting **[1]**. The population will not have enough resources to survive and breed **[1]**.

13. **(a)** Double blind

(b) This is a model answer which would score full marks:
Drug trials are designed to determine whether a drug works or not. They also show whether there are any side effects. With this particular trial, the drug had already been successfully tested on animals. The effect on humans could not have been predicted. Therefore the trial, although harming the volunteers, did prove that it was not safe to use on humans and so was a success. However, six of the volunteers suffered a violent reaction, had to be admitted to intensive care and nearly lost their lives.

(c) As they were raised in sterile conditions, the monkeys had not been exposed to disease **should be ticked.**

(d) $1.2 ÷ 500 = 0.0024$mg or 2.4μm

[1 for correct working but wrong answer]

14. **(a)**

How Water is Lost	Percentage	Volume of Water Lost Each Day (cm³)
Urine	40	1200
Faeces	5	150
Sweat	45	1350
Breathing	10	300

(b) (i) Anti-diuretic hormone / ADH

(ii) ADH production decreases

(iii) ADH production increases

Module B3: Life on Earth
(Pages 25–34)

1. **(a) Diagram A should be ticked.**

(b) The ability to breed and produce fertile offspring.

2. **(a)** Sparrows, mice and toads **[All three needed for 1 mark.]**

(b) Any one from: The grasshopper population will increase because there are fewer mice to eat them; The grasshopper population will decrease because other organisms that would have fed on the mice now feed on them.

(c) Any one from: The rabbit population will increase because there is more grass for them to eat, owing to fewer mice feeding on it; The rabbit population will decrease because there are fewer mice for hawks to eat, so they will attempt to compensate with other things they eat.

3. (a) Algae ⟶ Mayfly nymphs ⟶ Water beetles ⟶ Sticklebacks
   [1 for correct order; 1 for the arrows pointing in the correct direction]
   (b) Algae
   (c) Mayfly nymphs
   (d) Four
   (e) **Any two from:** Excreted waste; Respiration; Trapped in indigestible material; Movement of organisms
   (f) Decomposers

4. (a) 1 Combustion; 2, 3 and 4 Respiration **[all three needed for 1 mark]**; 5 Photosynthesis; 6 Death
   (b) All organic molecules contain carbon.

5. (a) Location A: 5.0(ppm); Location B: 40(ppm) **[Both needed for 1 mark.]**
   (b) **This is a model answer which would score full marks:**
   The evidence suggests that the nitrate levels are much higher at location B than at location A. The nitrate is polluting the river and has changed the conditions. Bloodworms and rat-tailed maggots are pollution-loving organisms. As they are found at location B, it confirms the presence of pollutants. At location A, organisms that can only live in unpolluted water are found. All organisms have different environmental preferences, so their presence or absence can indicate problems in the environment. This is a very quick technique that provides evidence without much disruption to the environment.

6. (a) 3500; radiological dating **and** many other **should be ringed.**
   (b) (i) Alan
   (ii) Becky

7. There is not enough evidence to reach a firm conclusion **should be ticked.**

8. (a) **Any one from:** Landfill sites; Incinerator plants
   (b) Because there is more waste at a landfill using up available oxygen, there is less available for the organisms that would break down the packaging.
   (c) **Any three from:** What materials should be used; How much energy is used; How much pollution will be produced; Time to rot; Release of chemicals; Effect on other organisms
   (d) The packaging is used to attract the customer to get them to buy the product.
   (e) Meeting the needs of people today without damaging the Earth for future generations

9. (a) Percentage of energy successfully transferred
   $$= \frac{\text{Amount used}}{\text{Amount potentially available}} \times 100$$
   $$= (90 \div 1000) \times 100$$
   $$= 9\%$$
   [1 for correct working but wrong answer]
   (b) **This is a model answer which would score full marks:**
   A proportion of the energy that comes from the Sun is captured and stored in the plant tissue. The caterpillar eats the plant and some of the energy is transferred. It is either stored in the caterpillar's body or lost through respiration, movement or keeping the caterpillar warm. The bird eats the caterpillar and stores some of the energy in its body. The rest, like in the caterpillar, is lost through respiration, movement or keeping the bird warm. Scientists are interested in this because they can determine the efficiency of a food web and better understand what will happen if parts of the food web are disturbed – for example, if new organisms are introduced or others are removed (by hunting or for food products).

10. The biologists did not look at other similar locations in the UK to see if the worms were affected in the same way **should be ticked.**

11. **Lines should be drawn from** Earthworm **and** Woodlouse **to** Detritivore. **[Both needed for 1 mark.]**
    Lines should be drawn from Bacteria **and** Fungus **to** Decomposer. **[Both needed for 1 mark.]**

12. (a) Nitrogen-fixing bacteria; Lightning strikes
    (b) Eaten by animals 4; Denitrifying bacteria 1; Nitrifying bacteria 3; Nitrogen-fixing bacteria 2 **[1 for each correct answer up to a maximum of 3.]**

13. **Any three from:** Mutations; Natural selection; Environmental change; Isolation

14. (a) The fossil record has gaps and lets us see what organisms were like at an earlier time.
    (b) **Any two from:** Fossils are formed randomly; Not every step in an organism's development is recorded in the fossil record; The bacteria were still alive but fossils are not.
    (c) A mutation must have occurred.
    (d) **This is a model answer which would score full marks:**
    Selective breeding is where a breeder selects breeding pairs based on the desired characteristics that an organism has. The genes are already present – they just need to be selected. If the genes were already there, however, then the new characteristic would turn up regularly whenever the conditions for expressing that characteristic were right. However, in Lenski's experiment, it only appeared in one flask. Furthermore, the gene for the new characteristic would have been detected in the original cultures if it were always there, so the gene must have arisen because of a new, random mutation. This means that evolution has taken place in the flask and not selective breeding.
    (e) Go back to an earlier generation and see if the same mutation occurs again **and** Use technology to see how the DNA has changed **should be ticked.**

Module C1: Air Quality
(Pages 35–45)

1. (a) A compound that contains only carbon and hydrogen.
   (b) Combustion **and** Oxidation **should be ticked.**
   (c)

   [1 for a correctly drawn CO_2 molecule; 1 for a correctly drawn H_2O molecule; 1 for showing one CO_2 molecule and two H_2O molecules]
   (d) There is a limited oxygen supply so carbon particulates and carbon monoxide may be produced.
   (e) **Any four from:** Fossil fuel sources will eventually run out so we need an alternative to power our cars; To reduce the atmospheric pollution caused by the combustion engine; To reduce the overall production of CO_2, which is a greenhouse gas; To improve the environment, e.g. reduce the amount of damage done to buildings by carbon particulates and acid rain; To help reach the Government's CO_2 reduction targets

2. (a) (i) cooled; condensed **[Both needed for 1 mark.]**
   (ii) photosynthesis; dissolving
   (iii) photosynthesis
   (b) Oxygen 21%; Nitrogen 78% **[Both needed for 1 mark.]**
   (c) **This is a model answer which would score full marks:**
   Changes in the composition of today's atmosphere resulting from human activity include the burning of fossil fuels in power stations and the combustion engine. When a fossil fuel burns, carbon dioxide and water vapour are released into the atmosphere. Many types of fossil fuel contain sulfur, which burns to produce sulfur dioxide.
   Deforestation is another example of how human activity is leading to increased levels of carbon dioxide in the atmosphere. Trees remove carbon dioxide by photosynthesis, thus lowering the levels. When trees are cut down they are sometimes burned as fuel, which adds more carbon dioxide to the atmosphere.

The occurrence of volcanic eruptions is an example of how natural causes are also changing the composition of today's atmosphere. Large volumes of volcanic ash and gases such as carbon dioxide, sulfur dioxide and water vapour enter the atmosphere.

3. (a) **Any suitable answer, e.g.** Generally, the sales of hay fever products increased when the pollen count increased and decreased when the pollen count decreased **[1]**. The sales peaked at the end of June after the pollen count had been at its highest, but in April, July and August sales did not increase as significantly as the pollen count **[1]**. The evidence is not conclusive because there are lots of variables such as temperature, humidity and other pollutants **[1]**.

   (b) When pollen was stuck to the skin of volunteers, some volunteers had an allergic reaction **[1]**. The results show that people with a pollen allergy also suffered from hay fever. Those that did not have a pollen allergy did not suffer from hay fever **[1]**.

   (c) Other scientists would study the data and repeat the skin tests **[1]**. The fact that the same results were always produced would prove that they were reliable **[1]**.

   (d) (i) That although nitrogen oxides can increase the chance of an asthma attack, it is not the only cause.
       (ii) What factors cause asthma; What factors make asthma worse

4. (a) Always driving to the shops **and** Buying a car with a bigger engine **should be ticked**.

   (b) (i) $2CO + O_2 \longrightarrow 2CO_2$
           [1 for correct formulae; 1 for balancing correctly]
       (ii) $2NO + 2CO \longrightarrow N_2 + 2CO_2$
           [1 for correct formulae; 1 for balancing correctly]

   (c) Fitting a filter system **and** Using hydroelectricity to power it **should be ticked**.

   (d) (i) **This is a model answer which would score full marks:**
           On a national level, new legislation was put into place. Legal limits have been set for vehicle exhaust emissions, which are enforced by the statutory MOT tests. This could have an impact on the local economy because, for example, garages would have to spend money updating their MOT testing systems. Also, catalytic converters have been made compulsory on new cars. This could have an impact on the local economy because new cars would need the latest technologies fitted, which may be more expensive.
           There are schemes in place to help and encourage people to insulate their homes. These will lead to lower energy use and more local work. Local councils have taken measures such as introducing doorstep collections of paper, bottles, metals and plastics for recycling. This could have an impact on the local economy because it may create more jobs. Local councils are also providing more regular bus services and introducing park-and-ride schemes. Again, these measures could create more local jobs.
       (ii) **Any suitable answer, e.g.** Different countries may take different action due to their specific circumstances **[1]**. For example, a mountainous country may invest in renewable energy such as hydroelectric power. A flat country may encourage people to cycle by developing a network of cycle paths around its cities **[1]**.

   (e) **Any suitable answer, e.g.** Individuals can recycle paper, bottles, metals, plastics and textiles. This helps to conserve natural resources and also saves energy **[1]**. People can turn off electrical appliances in their home, such as the TV, rather than leaving them on standby. This uses less energy and therefore reduces the demand for energy from power stations, which in turn reduces air pollution **[1]**.

5. (a) (i) **Any one from:** Carbon dioxide comes from burning fossil fuels in power stations; Carbon dioxide comes from burning fossil fuels in the combustion engine.

       (ii) Nitrogen monoxide is created because of the high temperatures in the combustion engine.
       (iii) Sulfur dioxide comes from burning coal and other fossil fuels in power stations and combustion engines.
       (iv) Carbon particulates come from the incomplete combustion of coal / fossil fuels.

   (b)

Name	Formula	Molecule
Carbon dioxide	CO_2	
Nitrogen monoxide	NO	
Water	H_2O	
Sulfur dioxide	SO_2	

   (c) **Lines should be drawn from** Carbon dioxide **to** Used by plants during photosynthesis; **from** Sulfur dioxide **to** Reacts with water to form acid rain; **from** Carbon particulates **to** Deposited on buildings **and from** Nitrogen oxides **to** Reacts with water to form acid rain. **[1 for each correct line.]**

   (d) (i) To make sure that the carbon monoxide levels do not get too high
       (ii) 5.2(ppm); 5.9(ppm) **[Both needed for 1 mark.]**

6. (a) The early atmosphere contained large amounts of water, carbon dioxide and ammonia **[1]**. Today's atmosphere contains large amounts of nitrogen, oxygen and a little carbon dioxide **[1]**.

   (b) As green plants started to grow the amount of carbon dioxide went down **[1]** and the amount of oxygen went up **[1]**. This is due to the fact that, during photosynthesis, plants take in carbon dioxide and give out oxygen **[1]**.

   (c) **Any suitable answer, e.g.** Scientists are worried that the composition of the atmosphere is changing due to human activity **[1]**. This in turn could have a massive impact on the environment, ultimately leading to climate change **[1]**. If scientists collect enough data to prove their theory, they will be able to put pressure on governments to make changes **[1]**. For example, if the levels of carbon dioxide are significantly higher in city centres, there is an argument for introducing congestion controls **[1]**.

7. (a) Variables (i.e. factors that change) affect concentrations, e.g. volume of traffic, weather conditions **[1]**; Accuracy of measuring equipment **[1]**; User's skill in using the measuring equipment and in recording the data accurately **[1]**

   (b) 0.3(ppm); 3.5(ppm) **[Both needed for 1 mark.]**

   (c) **Any three from:** To find the best estimate of the true value; To identify outliers; To allow discarding of outliers; To ensure that the results are reliable

   (d) 0.3(ppm)

   (e) Mean = Sum of all values ÷ Number of values
       Mean for town centre = (2.5 + 3.0 + 3.5) ÷ 3 = 3(ppm)
       The outlier has not been used in the calculation.
       [1 for correct working but wrong answer; 1 for excluding outlier]
       Mean for country park = (0.2 + 0.1 + 0.1 + 0.2) ÷ 4 = 0.15(ppm) **[1]**

   (f) The concentration of sulfur particles is significantly higher in the town centre **[1]**. The data supports the theory because there are more vehicles and buildings in the town centre than in the countryside **[1]**.

   (g) Yes, because the difference between the mean values is a lot greater than the range of each set of data **[1]**. If the difference between the mean values had been smaller than the range there would not have been a real difference. The result would have been insignificant and the data would not support the theory **[1]**.

8. (a) (i) The nitrogen and oxygen in the air react together **[1]** because of the high temperatures in the engines **[1]**.

(ii) Nitrogen monoxide **[1]**

[1 for correctly drawn NO molecules; 1 for balancing correctly]

(iii) Oxidation **should be ticked**.

(b) A mixture of nitrogen oxides **[1]**: NO and NO_2 **[1]**

(c) Nitrogen oxides are greenhouse gases **[1]** and cause acid rain **[1]**.

(d) Nitrogen; Carbon dioxide **[1]**

[1 for correctly drawn molecules; 1 for balancing correctly]

9. **(a)** Coal contains sulfur atoms **[1]**. During combustion the sulfur reacts with oxygen to form sulfur dioxide **[1]**.

(b) absorbed

(c) Sulfur dioxide is an acidic oxide **[1]** and when dissolved in water it forms acid rain **[1]**.

Module C2: Material Choices
(Pages 46–53)

1. **(a)**

Material	Natural Resources	Chemical Synthesis
Nylon		✓
Wood	✓	
PVC		✓
Wool	✓	

(b) Any suitable answer, e.g.

Material	Properties	Uses
Nylon	Lightweight Stretchy Strong Waterproof	**Any one from:** **Clothing** **Climbing ropes**
Wood	Quite a good insulator of heat Hard and rigid Waterproof	**Any one from:** **Fences** **Furniture**
PVC	High tensile strength Tough and durable Not very stretchy Waterproof	**Window frames**
Wool	Medium strength Good insulator of heat Stretchy Adsorbs water	**Any one from:** **Clothing** **Carpets**

[1 for each material]

(c) (i) To ensure that the results were reliable **[1]**; To find the best estimate of the true value to work out the mean value **[1]**; To identify any outliers **[1]**

(ii) 615.9(kN); 617.5(kN) **[Both needed for 1 mark.]**

2. **(a)** Fractional distillation **should be ticked**.

(b) Carbon; Hydrogen **[Both needed for 1 mark; no marks if any others listed.]**

(c) The strength of the forces between the hydrocarbon molecules increases as the length of the molecule increases **[1]**. More energy is needed to break the forces between the molecules in the liquid form to make a gas **[1]**. So, molecules with different lengths will evaporate at different temperatures, allowing the separation of the different hydrocarbons **[1]**.

3. **(a)** Gwyneth; Jonathan

(b) This is a model answer which would score full marks:
Suncream contains nanoparticles of titanium dioxide which

are very good at absorbing ultraviolet radiation, making the sunscreen more effective.
Many leading manufacturers of sports equipment have started adding nanoscale silicon dioxide crystals to tennis rackets. The resulting polymer gives better performance without changing the weight. The tennis rackets with silicon nanoparticles are stronger and more efficient.
[Other examples of products that use nanoparticles to change the properties of materials used to make the products are acceptable.]

(c) Nanotechnology is still in the early stages of development **[1]**. Some products are being put on the market before they have been fully tested **[1]**. It may take many years for any harmful health effects to become apparent and be linked to nanotechnology **[1]**.

4. **(a) This is a model answer which would score full marks:**
All three materials are strong enough for the children to sit on, so the class didn't think that strength was an important factor. Polypropene is cheaper than both wood and iron, however, so they will be able to buy more chairs with their money. Polypropene also has a low density so it will be easy to move the chairs around, whereas iron and wood may both be too heavy for the children to move on their own.

(b) Polypropene is made from a non-renewable material **and** Polypropene is non-biodegradable **should be ticked**.

(c) In strong winds a polypropene chair could be blown away but an iron one would not be **[1]**. This is because iron has a much higher density than polypropene **[1]**.

5. **(a)** C_2H_3Cl

(b) Monomers **should be ticked**.

(c) Small molecules **[1]** (called monomers) are joined together to make a long molecule / chain **[1]** called a polymer.

(d) Diagram C should be ticked.

(e) A plasticizer is a small molecule which sits between the polymer chains **[1]**. This forces the chains to be further apart **[1]**, which weakens the forces between the chains **[1]**, allowing the molecules to move more freely.

6. **(a) Diagram A should be ticked**.

(b) Cross-linking **should be ticked**.

(c) Vulcanised rubber is used to make car tyres because it has a higher tensile strength **[1]** and is harder **[1]** than naturally occurring rubber. This is because during vulcanisation strong cross-links are formed between the polymer chains **[1]**, so that they are no longer able to move **[1]** (see diagram B).

7. **(a) (i)** B – Buckminster fullerene should be ringed.

(ii) Any suitable answer, e.g. They have a much larger surface area to volume ratio **[1]** than larger particles of the same materials, which means they can be used to change existing properties **[1]**. For example, they can make polymers stronger **[1]**.

(b) (i) Any two from: Unreactive; Shiny; Does not react with water

(ii) Any two from: Antibiotics are more effective as they are easier to get into the body; Silver can be hard to remove from around the wound when the patient is better; If silver doesn't dissolve it will not get to the main problem area; Silver is expensive

(iii) This is a model answer which would score full marks:
When silver is applied directly to the wound, the particles are too large to be dissolved and absorbed directly into the body. The healing process is very slow. Nanoscale silver particles are very much smaller and have different properties due to the much larger surface area to volume ratio. Unlike the larger particles, the nanoscale particles can be absorbed directly into the body, making the healing process much quicker.

(iv) Any suitable answer, e.g. Inform the public that there are regulations for the development of new products **[1]**. Inform the public that reports by scientific advisors suggest that most nanotechnologies fit within the regulations [1]. Include a warning label saying that the long-term effects of exposure to a particular material are not known [1].

Module C3: Chemicals in Our Lives: Risks and Benefits (Pages 54–64)

1. (a) The Earth's crust is made up of large pieces of rocks called tectonic plates [1]. These move slowly across the Earth's surface [1].
    (b) **Any two from:** Africa and South America look like two pieces of a jigsaw; The same fossils have been found in different continents; There are magnetic clues left in the rocks that can track the movement of plates; The same rocks are found in different continents; Rocks in Britain have formed in different climatic regions.
    (c) (i) **Mountains form where the plates meet. This should be clearly marked on the diagram.**
        (ii) When two continental plates move towards each other [1], they are pushed upwards [1], forming mountains.
    (d) **This is a model answer which would score full marks:**
        As rocks are weathered small fragments are broken off. The fragments are broken down further as they are transported to different places by the process of erosion. Eventually the sediments enter the sea. Over the years, layers of sediments build up. Eventually the increased pressure causes minerals to be formed as the water is squeezed out. Eventually sandstone is formed. The process of sedimentation takes millions of years.

2. (a)

B	A	D	E	C

[1 for each correctly placed up to a maximum of 4.]
    (b) **Any three from:** Creates an ugly landscape; Produces noise and air pollution from the machinery and increased traffic; Destroys natural habitats; Creates dips on the surface where the ground is sinking
    (c) (i) Electrolysis **should be ringed.**
        (ii) Hydrogen, Chlorine **and** Sodium hydroxide **should be ticked. [All three needed for 1 mark.]**
        (iii) Chlorine is a toxic gas and could damage wildlife if there was a leak [1].
        Hydrogen is explosive and if set alight would do extensive damage to natural habitats [1].
        Sodium hydroxide is corrosive and will burn living tissue, which would damage wildlife if there was a leak [1].
        If other chemicals were ticked in part (ii), the following answers are acceptable:
        Hydrochloric acid is either corrosive or an irritant depending on concentration, so will harm living tissue [1].
        Sodium chlorate is corrosive, so can cause burns to living tissue and gives off a toxic gas if in contact with an acid [1].
        There are no real environmental concerns associated with water [1].
        [To gain each mark, the environmental effect of each product must be given.]

3. (a) Too much salt can lead to headaches **should be ticked.**
    (b) To improve the taste **and** To make the food last longer **should be ticked. [Both needed for 1 mark.]**
    (c) **Any two from:** Salt is a preservative [1] that allows processed foods to be kept longer. Food with less salt would have a shorter shelf life. This would mean that the processed foods would have to be replaced more regularly, which would cost the company more money [1]. Food with less salt may not taste as nice [1].
    (d) So that the public know what is in the food products [1] and so that they can calculate, for example, how much salt or how many calories they are eating each day [1].
    (e) They decide what must be put on food labels [1]; They carry out tests to ensure that the food is safe to eat [1]; They monitor the food industry to make sure that food companies are operating within the law [1].

4. (a) To encourage a reduction in waste [1]; To increase awareness of the environmental impact [1]
    (b) Making the material from raw materials, Manufacture, Use, Disposal **should be ticked.**
    (c) (i) Reusable nappies are better [1]. They produce a lot less waste than disposable nappies [1]. During manufacture they use less energy and raw materials [1] and less water is wasted [1].
        (ii) **Either disposable or reusable nappies will gain a mark but the choice must be supported by a suitable reason, e.g.** Most parents will choose disposable nappies because they are much more convenient to use; Most parents will choose reusable nappies because they are much better for the environment.

5. (a) Increases **should be ticked.**
    (b) Too much salt can increase the chance of a heart attack **should be ticked.**
    (c) (i) $1.1 + 0.2 + 1.8 + 0.7 + 0.2 = 4.0 (g)$
        (ii) $6.0 - 4.0 = 2.0 (g)$
        (iii) Abigail should have the beef burger and salad [1] because this would mean her salt intake for the day is still within the RDA [1], whereas the other meal would take her above the RDA.
    (d) **This is a model answer which would score full marks:**
        Salt is a preservative so the food will keep for longer. It can also add flavour to poor quality ingredients. Processed food is cheaper to buy than fresh ingredients and contains more salt. If less salt was used, the profits the restaurants make may decrease. The restaurants could increase their prices but this might reduce the number of customers.

6. (a) Burnt wood **and** Stale urine **should be ticked.**
    (b) (i) To neutralise acid soil
        (ii) To bind natural dyes to clothes
        (iii) To make glass
    (c) (i) Hydrogen chloride will form acid rain [1], which damages plants and buildings [1].
        Heaps of waste materials create an ugly landscape / destroy natural habitats [1].
        Hydrogen sulfide will poison living things [1].
        (ii) Pollution caused by a chemical can sometimes be addressed by a chemical reaction [1]. When a chemical reacts with something else, different compounds are made. These compounds will have different properties which may be harmless to the environment [1].
    (d) (i) Sodium chloride
        (ii) Sulfuric acid; Water **[Both needed for 1 mark.]**
        (iii) Nitric acid; Carbon dioxide **[Both needed for 1 mark.]**
    (e) Calcium carbonate will react with the acid rain [1] to produce a salt, water and carbon dioxide gas **[1 for products as words or equation for reaction]**. As a result, the limestone will wear away more quickly [1].

7. (a) To provide data about how many deaths from cancer there are that are a result of causes other than pollution, so that comparisons can be made
    (b) (i) It varied between about 50 and 60 deaths per hundred thousand people.
        (ii) It varied between about 90 and 105 deaths per hundred thousand people.
    (c) The study shows that there is a link between access to treated drinking water and the number of deaths from cancer [1]. Recommend further studies are carried out to confirm the results [1] and water treatment centres are built in the polluted and most polluted areas [1].
    (d) **This is a model answer which would score full marks:**
        In the previously polluted and most polluted areas, the number of deaths from cancer would be expected to have dropped to about the same as the control areas. However, the death rate in the control area may also have dropped due to other improvements such as greater access to medicines. The general health would be expected to have improved as a result of adding chlorine to the water, as chlorine kills many of

the microorganisms that are responsible for diseases (such as typhoid).

8. (a) **Any one from:** A solid crust formed; Mountains formed
    (b) Large slabs of rock that make up the Earth's crust and upper mantle
    (c) Africa and South America look like two pieces of a jigsaw; The same fossils are found in different continents **and** Magnetic clues left in the rocks can track the movement of plates **should be ticked**.
    (d) **Any two from:** They had not seen all the evidence; At the time it seemed a ridiculous theory because no one could actually see the plates moving; They couldn't explain why the plates would move; It went against the accepted theories of the day; It disagreed with biblical theories because this would make the Earth millions of years old.
    (e) **Any suitable answer, e.g.** When two plates collide as a result of moving towards each other **[1]**, huge pressures cause the rocks to fold and buckle **[1]**, resulting in the formation of mountains; When an oceanic plate and a continental plate collide **[1]** and the denser continental plate is forced down under the oceanic one **[1]**, new mountains are formed.
    (f) **This is a model answer which would score full marks:** Sedimentary rocks are made up from a range of different types of sediment, shown by the presence of fossils and shells. The types of fossil found in the different layers of rock would tell scientists about processes that took place a very long time ago. The Yorkshire Dales was once part of the marine environment and the sediments, including fish and broken shells, built up on the ocean bed. The ripple marks found in the rock show that the water was still there during the final stages of sedimentation.

Module P1: The Earth in the Universe (Pages 65–75)

1. (a) 4500 million years ago **should be ticked**.
    (b) **Any suitable answers, e.g.** There was no way of testing it; It was an old, established theory.

2. (a) 5(m)
    (b) Frequency = Speed ÷ Wavelength
    = 4 ÷ 10
    = 0.4(Hz)
    [1 for correct working but wrong answer]

3. (a) The theory of continental drift states that the continents were once joined together **[1]** but became separated and drifted apart **[1]**.
    (b) **This is a model answer which would score full marks:** Wegener saw that all the continents fitted together like a jigsaw, especially the coastlines of South America and Africa. Sedimentary rock formations in South America and Africa matched up. Also, fossils of the same land animals were found on different continents as well as living land animals today. Wegener's theory was rejected by many scientists because he wasn't a geologist and was treated as an outsider. The movement of the continents was not measurable at that time and a land bridge between continents provided a more likely explanation. Modern evidence of continental drift is provided by magnetic striping either side of the Mid-Atlantic Ridge as the seafloor spreads by a few centimetres each year.

4. (a) Tectonic plates **should be ticked**.
    (b) Earthquakes; Volcanoes; Mountain formations
    (c) liquid; Convection; tectonic; magma

5. Slide past each other; Move apart; Move towards each other (destructive)

6. (a) Plates sliding past each other
    (b) **Any two from:** At a constructive plate boundary the tectonic plates move apart; Molten rock rises to the surface, where it

solidifies to form new rock (seafloor spreading); The process is driven by convection currents in the mantle.
    1 mark for a suitable example, e.g. Oceanic ridges such as the Mid-Atlantic Ridge; the Rift Valley in Africa
    (c) **Any two from:** At a destructive plate boundary the tectonic plates move towards each other; One plate is forced under the other plate / The thinner, denser oceanic plate is forced under the thicker continental plate; Earthquakes and volcanoes are common.
    1 mark for a suitable example, e.g. The west coast of South America
    (d) The oceanic plate is forced under the continental plate; Melting / Subduction occurs
    (e) Tectonic plates are less dense than the mantle and therefore float on top **should be ticked**.

7. (a) gas; gravity; heat; fusion
    (b) **Lines should be drawn from** Asteroids **to** Small rocky masses that orbit the Sun; **from** Comets **to** Small icy masses that orbit the Sun; **from** Dwarf planets **to** Large masses that have not cleared their orbits of other objects; **from** Moons **to** Rocky masses that orbit planets; **and from** Planets **to** Large masses that orbit the Sun. **[1 for each correct line up to a maximum of 4.]**
    (c)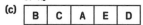
    [1 for each correctly placed up to a maximum of 4.]

8. (a) About 5000 million years old
    (b) Energy is released during the process of nuclear fusion **[1]**. Lighter elements such as hydrogen atoms fuse to make new heavier elements such as helium **[1]**.
    (c) Our galaxy contains at least 100 billion stars **should be ticked**.
    (d)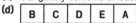
    [1 for each correctly placed up to a maximum of 4.]
    (e) A light-year is the distance light travels in one year **[1]** (approximately 9500 billion kilometres). Scientists use light-years to measure distances in space because they are so vast **[1]**.
    (f) The light we see today left the galaxy 2.2 million years ago **[1]**. We are therefore seeing the galaxy as it was in the past **[1]**.
    (g) Relative brightness; Parallax

9. **Any three from:** Visible light; Ultraviolet; Infrared; Gamma; X-rays; Microwave; Radio

10. Light pollution is the effect of the electric lights that illuminate the night sky and make it difficult to see the stars.

11. (a) That the Universe started with a huge explosion
    (b) 14 000 million years

12. (a) energy; matter; energy; travels
    (b) (i) For a longitudinal wave the pattern of disturbance is in the same direction as the direction of the wave movement **[1]**, while for a transverse wave the pattern of disturbance is at right angles to the direction of wave movement **[1]**.
        (ii) Longitudinal: sound waves; Transverse: light / water waves
    (c) (i) The number of waves produced / passing a particular point in one second
        (ii) Hertz

13. (a) Robert
    (b) There is a very large number of hydrogen nuclei **[1]** and therefore the total amount of energy released is very large **[1]**.
    (c) **This is a model answer which would score full marks:** All stars have a finite life span. They obtain their energy from converting hydrogen into helium in nuclear fusion. Eventually hydrogen supplies run out and they begin to convert helium into heavier elements, such as carbon and lithium. Massive stars eventually explode in a supernova during which the very heavy elements, such as gold, are formed.

14. **(a)** and **and** but not **should be ringed**.
    (b) **(i)** All the points, A, B, C, D, E, F and G
        (ii) A, B, F and G
    (c) Waves are refracted gradually **[1]** because they change speed as the density changes gradually **[1]**.
    (d) Waves are refracted suddenly **[1]** at a change in material, where their speed changes suddenly **[1]**.

15. **This is a model answer which would score full marks:**
    The Earth has a magnetic field. The polarity of the field changes approximately every one million years. New rock is formed at constructive plate boundaries where the plates are moving apart. As the rock cools, the polarity of the Earth's magnetic field is set in the solid rock. This produces stripes of alternating polarity. Geologists can use this to estimate how quickly new rock is formed and therefore how quickly tectonic plates are moving. An example would be the Mid-Atlantic Ridge.

16. **This is a model answer which would score full marks:**
    Tectonic plates move due to convection currents in the mantle. Old rock is destroyed through subduction. Igneous rock is formed when magma reaches the surface. Plate collisions produce high pressure and temperatures, which can cause folding and change sedimentary rock into metamorphic rock.

17. Most galaxies appear to be red shifted and the more distant a galaxy is, the more it is red shifted, which means that they are moving away from us **[1]**. If they are moving away from us, then the Universe is expanding **[1]**.

18. **(a)** The amount of mass in the Universe.
    (b) 'Big crunch': Too much mass
        Expand forever: Not enough mass

19. **(a)** **Lines should be drawn from** P-wave **to** Longitudinal **and from** S-wave **to** Transverse.
    (b) The speed is greater in the mantle because it is denser than the crust **[1]**. Mechanical waves travel more quickly through denser materials **[1]** as the particles are closer together and the vibrations are passed on more quickly **[1]**.
    (c) P-wave: time = 40 ÷ 6 = 6.7(s)
        S-wave, time = 40 ÷ 4 = 10(s)
        10 − 6.7 = 3.3(s)
        [All correct for 3 marks; 1 for correct working but wrong answer]

Module P2: Radiation and Life (Pages 76–85)

1. **(a)** Photons **should be ticked**.
   (b) Microwaves: D; Infrared: C; X-rays: B; Gamma rays: A **[1 for each correct up to a maximum of 3.]**

2. **(a)** **Any four suitable pairs, e.g.** Emitter: Sun, Detector: The eye; Emitter: Remote control, Detector: Television; Emitter: Stars, Detector: Gamma ray telescope; Emitter: X-ray machine, Detector: Photographic plate **[1 for each correct pair.]**
   (b) reflected; absorbed; transmitted **[1 for each correct up to a maximum of 2.]**

3. **(a)** Increase the distance between the source and the object; Place a material which absorbs the radiation between the source and the object.
   (b) The number of photons; The energy of each photon

4. **(a)** Tom; Jack
   (b) Anna
   (c) Grace; Emily

5. Ionising radiation can break molecules into bits called ions **and** X-rays and gamma rays are types of ionising radiation **should be ticked**.

6. **(a)** Surrounding nuclear reactors with lead **and** Wire screens in microwave ovens **should be ticked**.
   (b) Ionising radiation can damage cells; Ionising radiation can cause mutations which can lead to cancer.
   (c) By causing the water particles **[1]** in materials to vibrate **[1]**

7. **(a)** More heat will be absorbed by the atmosphere **should be ticked**.
   (b) photosynthesis; decreases **and** increases **should be ringed**.

8. **(a)** Less heat escapes back into space
   (b) Methane; Carbon dioxide; Water vapour

9. **This is a model answer which would score full marks:**
   Ozone is part of the atmosphere. The ozone layer absorbs some of the ultraviolet radiation from the Sun before it reaches the Earth. Ultraviolet radiation can be harmful if too much reaches the Earth's surface as it increases the risk of skin cancer.

10. **(a)** Eating of plants: D; Photosynthesis: B; Respiration: A; Death of plants and animals: C **[1 for each correct up to a maximum of 3.]**
    (b) Photosynthesis **[1]** by plants **[1]**
    (c) **This is a model answer which would score full marks:**
        The carbon obtained by photosynthesis is used to make carbohydrates, fats and proteins in plants. When the plants are eaten by animals, this carbon becomes carbohydrates, fats and proteins in the animals. Animals respire, releasing carbon dioxide back into the atmosphere.
    (d) The amount of carbon dioxide added to the atmosphere (by burning, respiration, etc.) **[1]** was roughly the same as the amount of carbon dioxide removed from the atmosphere by the process of photosynthesis **[1]**.
    (e) **This is a model answer which would score full marks:**
        Burning fossil fuels releases previously trapped carbon dioxide into the atmosphere. Deforestation is the removal of trees and this decreases the amount of carbon dioxide that is taken out of the atmosphere by photosynthesis.

11. **(a)** They have higher energy **and** They are not significantly refracted by the atmosphere **should be ticked**.
    (b) **(i)** X-rays
        (ii) Radio waves
        (iii) Microwaves
        (iv) **Any one from:** Light; Infrared
    (c) X-rays are absorbed by dense materials but can travel through less dense materials **[1]**. X-rays can cause changes in photographic film **[1]**.

12. **(a)** Frequency **and** Amplitude **should be ticked**.
    (b) A receiver decodes the pattern of variation **[1]** and reproduces the original sound **[1]**.

13. **(a)** An analogue signal can take any value, whereas a digital signal can only take two values, 0 or 1.
    (b) **(i)** False
        (ii) True
        (iii) True
        (iv) True
    (c) **(i)**

[1 for graph involving only vertical and horizontal lines; 1 for correct pattern of 0 and 1. Any height for the value of 1 and any width can be used so long as they are constant.]

(ii) Any suitable answer, e.g.

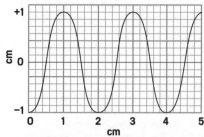

[1 for correct wavelength (2cm on horizontal axis for one complete wave); 1 for correct amplitude (1cm on vertical axis from the undisturbed position to *either* a peak *or* a trough)]

(d) Unwanted electrical interference

(e) A received analogue signal

14. Photons spread out; Photons are absorbed by particles; Photons are reflected by particles.

15. **Any one from:** duration; time

16. very reactive **and** can **should be ringed.**

17. **(a) Any two from:** Apply sun lotion; Wear clothing that covers the skin; Stay indoors

    (b) Sunburn and skin cancer

18. **(a)** Computer climate models **[1]** show that one of the main factors responsible for global warming is the rise in atmospheric carbon dioxide and other greenhouse gases **[1]**. This increase is caused by human activity such as deforestation **[1]**. **[Any suitable example can be given for 1 mark.]**

    (b) This is a model answer which would score full marks: Burning forests increases the amount of carbon dioxide in the atmosphere. This is because combustion releases carbon dioxide more quickly than respiration and natural decomposition would. Also, photosynthesis by plants absorbs carbon dioxide from the atmosphere, so their removal means that less carbon dioxide is absorbed.

19. **(a) This is a model answer which would score full marks:** Digital signals have two states, on and off, which can still be recognised despite any noise that is picked up. Therefore, it is easy to remove the noise / clean up the signal / restore the on/off pattern. Analogue signals have many different values, so it is hard to distinguish between noise and the original signal. This means that the noise cannot be completely removed and when the signal is amplified, any noise picked up is also amplified.

    (b) (i) Both
    (ii) Digital
    (iii) Digital
    (iv) Analogue

Module P3: Sustainable Energy (Pages 86–96)

1. **(a)** A magnet **[1]** rotates near a coil **[1]**.
   (b) (i) Potential energy; PE to kinetic energy; KE to Electrical **[All three needed for 2 marks. 1 mark for 'KE to Electrical'.]**
   (ii) Current = Power rating in watts ÷ Voltage
   = 36 ÷ 12 = 3(amps)
   [1 for correct working but wrong answer]
   (iii) Energy used = Power rating × Time in seconds
   = 36 × 20 × 60 = 43 200 (joules)
   [1 for correct working but wrong answer]
   (c) (i) Cindy
   (ii) Alex

2. **(a)** Electrical **should be ticked.**
   (b) It has to be produced from another (primary) energy source.

3. **(a)** Coal:
   Any one from: Emission of carbon dioxide; Emission of sulfur dioxide; Emission of particulates; Contributes to global warming / climate change; Not renewable
   Nuclear power:
   Any one from: Disposal of nuclear waste; Possibility of radioactive contamination; Perceived threat to the public; Power stations need a water supply
   (b) This is a model answer which would score full marks: Two possible alternative energy sources are wind and wave. Neither of these alternative sources emit any greenhouse gases or any gases that cause acid rain. Nor do they release particulates into the atmosphere. They are both renewable sources of energy. Neither generates nuclear waste, which is hazardous to both process and dispose of safely, nor do they emit radiation which can cause damage to living cells. **[Coastal areas are typical sites for tidal, wave and wind for obvious reasons, so these should be expected to be seen as answers with the advantages stated as above. Hydroelectric is unlikely to be suitable, as valleys that can be dammed are not necessarily near the coast. Solar is not necessarily suitable as it depends on the latitude of the location. Biomass requires large land area for production and coastal areas are usually prime real estate, so it would be very expensive to use land for biomass. Inland sites would be better. Geothermal is very dependent on location, so the coast is not necessarily the best place.]**

4. **(a)** Heat
   (b) 5%
   (c) Any one from: Gas; Coal; Oil
   (d) 55J **should be ringed.**

5. Energy is released from the nucleus. Heat is used to produce steam. Steam turns a turbine. The turbine drives the generator **should be ticked.**

6. Drawing a larger current from the generator would use up more petrol each second **should be ticked.**

7. **Lines should be drawn from** Wind farm **to** Are there any hills to cause turbulence?; **from** Biofuel **to** Is there sufficient farmland available?; **and from** Hydroelectric power **to** Is there a suitable place for a dam?
   [1 for each correct line up to a maximum of 2.]

8. **(a)** Use of more efficient appliances; Installation of loft insulation
   (b) Saving by use of more efficient appliances (condensing boiler) = 3 × £190 = £570
   Saving by installation of loft insulation = 3 × £145 = £435
   Total savings = £570 + £435 = £1005
   [1 for correct working but wrong answer]
   (c) Any one from: There is less wasted energy in the form of heat to pay for when using low energy bulbs; Low energy bulbs need to be replaced less often than normal ones.
   (d) This is a model answer which would score full marks: New products are made from raw materials and require energy to be used at each stage of the manufacturing process. Recycling will cut down on the number of new products required and therefore saves energy. Also, there will be less money spent and less energy wasted on disposal to landfill sites.

9. Supplies of coal from British mines ran out in the 1990s **and** The use of hydroelectric power increased after 1990 due to increased rainfall **should be ticked.**

10. **(a)** Units used in kWh = Power rating × Time
    = 0.1 × 8 = 0.8kWh
    Cost = Units used in kWh × Cost per unit
    = 0.8 × 8 = 6.4p
    [1 for correct working but wrong answer]

(b) Efficiency = Useful energy transferred ÷ Energy in × 100%
= 1800 ÷ 3000 × 100% = 60%
[1 for correct working but wrong answer]

11. **(a)** **(i)** **Any suitable answer, e.g.** People changed from using coal (fires) to gas (central heating). **['Gas was a more convenient source of energy than coal, which had to be stored on site' is also acceptable.]**

(ii) The mass of coal mined has remained constant since 2000.

(b) There is no data for the years in between the ones on the chart, so conclusions are made on limited information.

12. **This is a model answer which would score full marks:**
Biofuels and solar panels would both require large areas of land to produce sufficient energy. Burning biofuels also leads to greenhouse gas emissions and the production of particulates. Solar panels are expensive and the level of sunlight is not constant, so output can vary. Wind turbines, on the other hand, require low maintenance and emit no greenhouse gases or particulates. There may be some days without wind but not enough for the disadvantages to outweigh the advantages.

13. **Lines should be drawn from** Solar **to** It is ideal if the panels face south; **from** Hydroelectric **to** A dam needs to be built across a river **and from** Wind **to** Build in exposed areas.
[1 for each correct line up to a maximum of 2.]

14. **(a)** Fossil fuels (e.g. coal):
Any advantage from: Convenient to use; Easy to transport; Power stations can be built anywhere; High energy output
Any disadvantage from: Emission of carbon dioxide; Emission of sulfur dioxide; Emission of particulates; Contributes to global warming / climate change; Non-renewable
Nuclear fuel:
Any advantage from: Convenient to use; Easy to transport; High energy output; No emission of greenhouse gases; No emission of particulates; Reliable energy source
Any disadvantage from: Nuclear waste difficult to dispose of; Radioactivity from the fuel rods and spent fuel; Perceived threat to the public; Power stations need a water supply.

(b) **(i)** Wind turbines have a low power output, so you need a lot of wind turbines to match the output of a conventional power station; It is not always windy, so power output is not reliable.

(ii) **Any two advantages from:** Out of sight so little visual pollution; Windy locations; No buildings or hills to cause turbulence
Any two disadvantages from: Expensive to build; Inaccessible for repair; Long cables needed to transport electricity inland; Danger to shipping

(iii) **Any two from:** Hydroelectric; Wave; Tidal

15. **(a)** Solar energy:
Any one from: The intensity of light from the Sun varies and so the output from the solar panels will also vary; The intensity of sunlight in the UK is never large. This means that solar will not be able to supply the required quantity of electrical energy.
Wind power: It is not always windy so some days will give little energy output.

(b) The cost and supply of gas is controlled by other countries. This means that the UK's energy supply could be affected by world affairs.

(c) **This is a model answer which would score full marks:**
Alternative energy is a developing area but cannot provide all of the energy that the UK needs at the moment, although it can make a significant contribution. Solar and wind sources are unreliable and their output of energy is small compared to the needs of the National Grid. Hydroelectric power stations are expensive to build and there are only a few suitable sites for them. This means that fossil fuels and nuclear power must provide the bulk of our energy needs. The UK has coal, so has control of that energy source as it

does with wind and hydroelectric. Nuclear fuels come from stable areas of the world, but some of the gas and oil needed does not and they are expensive to import. It makes sense not to rely on one source.

16. **(a)** Rate = Energy in ÷ Time in seconds
= 10 000 ÷ 25 = 400(J/s or W)
[1 for correct working but wrong answer]

(b) **(i)** Current = Power rating ÷ Voltage
= 1150 ÷ 230 = 5 (amps)
[1 for correct working but wrong answer]

(ii) Energy transferred = Power rating × Time in seconds
= 1150 × 3 × 60 = 207 000 (joules)
[1 for correct working but wrong answer]

(iii) Units used = Power rating in kW × Time in hours
= 1.150 × (3 ÷ 60) = 0.0575(kWh)
[1 for correct working but wrong answer]

(iv) Total cost = Units used × Cost per unit
= 0.0575 × 8 = 0.46p
[1 for correct working but wrong answer]

(c) **(i)** Useful power output = (Percentage efficiency ÷ 100) × Power rating in watts
= (65 ÷ 100) × 2000 = 1300(W)
[1 for correct working but wrong answer]

(ii) Useful work done = Useful power out × Time in seconds = 1300 × 5 × 60 = 390 000 (joules)
[1 for correct working but wrong answer]

(d) Put a tick (✓) in the box next to the diagram that correctly represents part of a PVC molecule. [1]

A ⬡⬡⬡◯◯◯ ☐   C ◯⬡◯⬡⬡◯ ☐

B ⬡◯◯◯◯◯ ☐   D ◯⬡◯◯⬡◯ ☐

(e) Sometimes manufacturers want to make PVC more flexible, for example so that it can be used to make clothes. They do this by adding a small molecule called a plasticizer. Explain how a plasticizer works. [3]

....

....

....

....

....

6. In industry, the properties of a material are often modified to meet the needs of the application. Naturally occurring rubber used for erasers and rubber bands is soft and weak; vulcanised rubber used for car tyres and shock absorbers is hard and strong.

(a) Which diagram best represents the molecules found in naturally occurring rubber? Put a tick (✓) in the box next to the correct answer. [1]

A ☐   B ☐

(b) During vulcanisation, sulfur is added to the rubber. What process takes place as a result of this? Put a tick (✓) in the box next to the correct answer. [1]

Polymerisation ☐

Cross-linking ☐

Distillation ☐

Cracking ☐

(c) Explain why we use vulcanised rubber to make car tyres. You may wish to refer to the diagrams given in part **(a)**. [4]

....

....

....

....

7. Nanotechnology is the science of building things on a very tiny scale. Nanoscale materials are designed to do a specific job.

(a) (i) Different objects are different sizes. Put a ring around the object which is the size of a nanometre. [1]

A Earth

B Buckminster fullerene

C Bacterium

D Football field

(ii) Suggest reasons why nanoscale particles are so useful. [3]

....

....

....

....

(b) It is well known that silver has been used for jewellery, coins and decoration for centuries. However, not so many people know that silver was used by the ancient Greeks to purify water and that doctors used to apply a thin layer to wounds to prevent infection and help healing. When antibiotics were invented, doctors stopped using silver to treat wounds. Today, however, dressings containing nanoscale silver particles are being used on patients.

(i) What properties of silver make it good for jewellery? [2]

(ii) Suggest why doctors stopped using silver when antibiotics were invented. [2]

(iii) Suggest why doctors prefer using dressings containing nanoscale silver particles to applying silver directly to the wound.

The quality of written communication will be assessed in your answer to this question. [6]

(iv) Some people are worried about the long-term effects of nanotechnology on human health. Suggest what actions could be taken to address these concerns. [3]

[Total: ...... / 31]

1. People used to believe that features on the Earth's surface were caused by shrinkage when the Earth cooled following its formation. As scientists found out more about the Earth, this theory has been rejected and replaced by tectonic theory.

   (a) Explain what is meant by **tectonic theory**. [2]

   ....

   ....

   ....

   (b) What evidence have scientists found to support tectonic theory? [2]

   ....

   ....

   ....

   (c) (i) Mark clearly on the diagram below where you think that mountains could be formed. [1]

   Continental plate   Continental plate

   Cool mantle
   sinks

   (ii) Explain your answer to part (i). [2]

   ....

   ....

   ....

   ....

(d) The rock cycle plays an important role in the formation of mineral wealth in Britain. There are large deposits of sandstone, a sedimentary rock, found throughout the country.

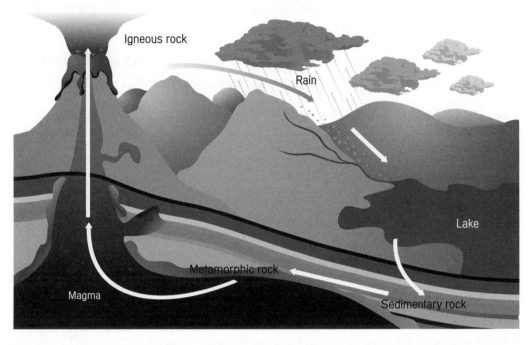

Study the diagram of the rock cycle and then explain how sandstone was formed.

✎ *The quality of written communication will be assessed in your answer to this question.* [6]

....

....

....

....

....

....

....

....

2. Salt deposits are found in several areas of Britain. Two different processes are used to extract salt from underground deposits. One method involves mining solid rock salt and is used when the salt is going to be used to treat roads in winter. The other involves solution mining and is used when other chemicals are going to be extracted from the salt.

(a) Here are some statements about the process of mining solid rock salt. They are not in the correct order. Put the statements in the correct order by writing the letters in the empty boxes. [4]

A The rock salt is loaded into a crusher, where it is ground up into small pieces.

B Explosives are used to blast the layer of exposed rock.

C The salt is put into large storage areas.

D A conveyor belt transports the salt to the lift shaft.

E The rock salt is transferred to hoppers and taken to the surface.

Start

B	i			

(b) What effects do this type of mining have on the environment? [3]

_____

_____

_____

_____

(c) In one major industrial process, an electric current is passed through an aqueous solution of sodium chloride to produce three important chemicals.

(i) What is the name of this process? Put a ring around the correct answer. [1]

Hydrogenation   **Electrolysis**   **Distillation**   **Oxidation**

(ii) Which three chemicals are made during this process? Put ticks (✓) in the boxes next to the **three** correct answers. [1]

Hydrogen ☐   Water ☐

Hydrochloric acid ☐   Chlorine ☐

Sodium chlorate ☐   Sodium hydroxide ☐

(iii) Salt is used in many industries to manufacture a range of different products such as disinfectants, soaps, ceramics, plastics, PVC and margarine. What are the environmental concerns associated with the chemicals you selected in part **(ii)** that are produced from salt in the manufacture of these products? [3]

....

....

....

....

....

3. Salt is an important component of a healthy diet. However, too much salt is not good for you. The Government recommends that an adult should eat 6g of salt a day. Experts estimate that most adults eat between 9g and 10g a day.

(a) The following are statements about salt. Put a tick (✓) in the box next to the statement that is **incorrect**. [1]

Salt is needed to maintain the correct concentration of fluids in the body. ☐

Too much salt can lead to headaches. ☑

Salt in the diet adds taste to food. ☐

Salt plays an important role in the transmission of electrical impulses in the nerves. ☐

(b) Why do food companies add salt to their products? Put ticks (✓) in the boxes next to the **two** correct answers. [1]

To improve the taste ☑

To make the food more healthy ☐

To make the food last longer ☑

To help the cooking process ☐

(c) Eating too much salt increases the risk of heart disease, high blood pressure and strokes. Explain why food companies may not want to lower the amount of salt in their products. [2]

....

....

....

(d) Suggest why it is important to have clear labels on food products. [2]

....

....

(e) How do government departments such as the Department of Health and the Department for Environment, Food and Rural Affairs help to make sure that food is safe, healthy and fairly marketed? [3]

....

....

....

....

4. Every new product has to undergo a life cycle assessment (LCA) that comprises four phases.

(a) What is the purpose of a life cycle assessment? [2]

....

....

....

(b) What are the four phases in a life cycle assessment? Put a tick (✓) in the box next to the correct answer. [1]

Manufacture, Use, Cost, Disposal ☐

Development, Making the material from raw materials, Manufacture, Disposal ☐

Making the material from raw materials, Manufacture, Use, Disposal ☐

Manufacture, Desirability, Use, Disposal ☐

(c) All babies need to use nappies and parents have to decide whether to use disposable nappies or reusable nappies. Disposable nappies are made from cellulose fibres, a super-absorbent polymer, whilst reusable ones are made from cloth. To help parents decide, the results of a life cycle assessment are readily available.

Impact (per baby, per year)	Disposable Nappies	Reusable Nappies
Energy needed to produce product	8900MJ	2532MJ
Waste water	28m³	12.4m³
Raw materials used	569kg	29kg
Domestic solid waste produced	361kg	4kg

(i) Using the information in the table, which type of nappy is better for the environment? You must give reasons for your answer. [4]

_____

_____

_____

_____

(ii) Which type of nappy do you think most parents choose? Why do you think they make this choice? [1]

_____

_____

_____

[Total: _____ / 42]

Higher Tier

5. The recommended daily allowance (RDA) of salt is as follows:

A baby from 0 to 12 months	1g salt per day
A child from 1 to 11 years	2–6g salt per day
An adult	6g salt per day

(a) As a child grows up, what happens to the RDA of salt? Put a tick (✓) in the box next to the correct answer. [1]

Stays the same ⬜   Increases ☑   Decreases ⬜

(b) The RDA for an adult with high blood pressure is less than 6g salt per day. Which statement best explains why? Put a tick (✓) in the box next to the correct answer. [1]

Salt is needed to help cells take up nutrients. ⬜

Too much salt makes you thirsty. ⬜

Too much salt can increase the chance of a heart attack. ⬜

Salt stops food from going off. ⬜

(c) Abigail is 11 years old. This is what she has eaten so far today:

Breakfast   2 crumpets containing a total of 1.1g of salt

              Spread containing 0.2g of salt

Lunch   200g of baked beans containing a total of 1.8g of salt

              2 slices of toast containing a total of 0.7g of salt

              Spread containing 0.2g of salt

(i) Calculate how much salt she has eaten today.   [1]

    4g

    1.1 + 0.2 + 1.8 + 0.7 + 0.2 = 4

                                                                       g

(ii) If Abigail is going to keep to her RDA of salt, how much salt can she have in her
     evening meal?   [1]

        2

                                                                       g

(iii) Abigail goes out for her evening meal. She can't decide whether to have a beef burger and
      salad, which contain a total of 1.9g of salt, or chicken tikka masala and rice, which contain
      a total of 3.5g of salt. Suggest, with a reason, which meal she should choose.   [2]

    She should chooze the burger with
    Salad because it has less salt and will
    keep her within the RDA

(d) Suggest, with reasons, why some high street restaurants serve meals with more than
    double the RDA of salt.

    ✐ The quality of written communication will be assessed in your answer to this question. [6]

6. Alkalis have always been very important chemicals, even before industrialisation.

(a) What were the traditional sources of alkalis? Put ticks (✓) in the boxes next to the **two** correct answers. [2]

Sandstone ☐   Iron ore ☐

Burnt wood ☐   Stale urine ✓

(b) Traditionally, why was it important for the following industries to have a good source of alkali?

(i) The farming industry: _____ [1]

(ii) The textile industry: _____ [1]

(iii) The building industry: _____ [1]

(c) In the 19th century, scientists had to start looking for ways to manufacture alkali to meet growing demand. Early attempts at producing alkali were successful but led to other problems.

The production of alkali from limestone and salt caused the following problems:

- Large volumes of acidic hydrogen chloride gas as a by-product

- Large heaps of waste material

- Foul smelling toxic fumes of hydrogen sulfide from the waste material

Scientists tried to overcome some of these problems by carrying out investigations into the reactions of the by-products.

(i) What was the environmental impact of each of the problems caused by the production of alkali from limestone and salt? [4]

_____

(ii) Suggest why scientists decided to investigate the by-products. [2]

_____

(d) Alkalis react with acids to produce a salt and water. Complete the following word equations.

    (i) Sodium hydroxide + Hydrochloric acid ⟶ _Salt_ + Water   [1]

    (ii) Potassium hydroxide + _____ ⟶ Potassium sulfate + _____   [1]

    (iii) Sodium carbonate + _____ ⟶ Sodium nitrate + Water + _____   [1]

(e) In areas where acid rain is frequent, limestone (calcium carbonate) gravestones suffer more weathering than in other areas. Explain why this happens.   [3]

_____

_____

_____

_____

7. The rapid expansion of China's economy, industrialisation and urbanisation, together with a lack of investment in basic water supplies and water treatment, led to widespread water pollution in the 1970s and 1980s. Since then, improvements have been made in many areas but up to a third of the population still do not have access to clean drinking water.

The bar chart below shows the results of a study of water pollution and human health carried out between 1975 and 1986. The people in the control area had access to treated drinking water.

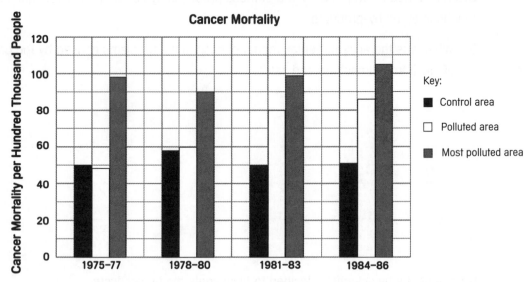

(a) Why did each part of the study include a control area?   [1]

_____

_____

(b) During the period of the study, how did the number of people dying from cancer change in…

    (i) the control areas? _____ [1]

    (ii) the most polluted areas? _____ [1]

(c) What conclusions can be drawn from the study and what recommendations could be made to the Chinese government? [3]

_____

_____

_____

_____

(d) Twenty years later, the people who carried out the original study revisited some of the previously 'polluted' and 'most polluted' areas. They found that the people living in these areas now had access to drinking water that had been treated with chlorine. Suggest, with reasons, how the number of people dying from cancer and the general health of the population might have changed. Explain your answer.

    🖉 *The quality of written communication will be assessed in your answer to this question.* [6]

_____

_____

_____

_____

_____

_____

8. Many years ago, people used to believe that mountains were formed because the Earth had shrunk in size as it cooled down. Scientists now think that mountains are formed as a result of moving tectonic plates.

(a) Suggest why scientists thought that the Earth had shrunk in size. [1]

_____

(b) What are tectonic plates? [1]

_____

(c) What three pieces of evidence suggest that tectonic plates move? Put ticks (✓) in the boxes next to the **three** correct answers. [3]

The rocks in each continent are very different. ☐

Africa and South America look like two pieces of a jigsaw. ☐

The same fossils are found in different continents. ☐

The same animals are found in different continents. ☐

Britain has a similar climate to Iceland. ☐

Magnetic clues left in the rocks can track the movement of plates. ☐

(d) At first, many scientists did not accept the theory of continental drift. Why was this? [2]

....

....

(e) Mountains are thought to form as a result of tectonic plate movement. Explain how this happens. [2]

....

....

....

....

(f) Limestone is a sedimentary rock found in the Yorkshire Dales. When the limestone was studied by geologists they found fossils of fish, fragments of shells and water ripple marks in the rock. What does this evidence tell us about how the limestone was formed?

✏ *The quality of written communication will be assessed in your answer to this question.* [6]

....

....

....

....

....

....

....

[Total: .... / 56]

1. **(a)** How long ago do scientists think the Earth was formed? Put a tick (✓) in the box next to the correct answer. [1]

   3500 million years ago ⬜

   4500 million years ago ⬜

   4000 million years ago ⬜

   4500 years ago ⬜

   (b) Some people used to believe that the Earth was only 6000 years old. Suggest **two** reasons for this. [2]

   1. ....

   2. ....

2. **(a)** The diagram shows a wave. What is the wavelength of this wave? [1]

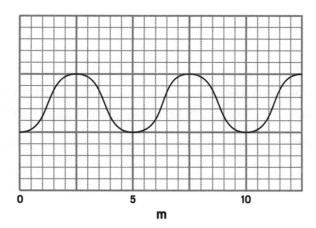

   .... m

   (b) Another wave has a wavelength of 10 metres and a speed of 4m/s. Calculate its frequency. [2]

   ....

   ....

   .... Hz

3. Alfred Wegener proposed the theory of continental drift.

How it once was   **How it is today**

Laurasia

Gondwanaland

(a) Briefly outline the theory of continental drift.   [2]

....

....

....

....

(b) Describe the evidence that Wegener put forward to support his theory and explain why many scientists did not accept this theory until further evidence was available.

✎ *The quality of written communication will be assessed in your answer to this question.*   [6]

....

....

....

....

....

....

....

....

....

4. **(a)** What do scientists call the large pieces of rock that the Earth's crust is cracked into? Put a tick (✓) in the box next to the correct answer. [1]

Convection plates ⬭

Conduction plates ⬭

Tectonic plates ⬭

Tectonic zones ⬭

(b) What **three** major features can occur at plate boundaries? [3]

1. ....

2. ....

3. ....

(c) Complete the following description of how the seafloor spreads. Use words from this list. [4]

tectonic   **liquid**   **constructive**   **magma**   **convection**

Just below the crust the mantle is fairly solid. However, further down it is

.... and able to move. .... currents in the

mantle carry the .... plates, moving entire continents. Where these

currents cause plates to move apart, ... rises to the surface and new

areas of oceanic crust are formed.

5. State **three** ways in which tectonic plates can move at a plate boundary. [3]

1. ....

2. ....

3. ....

6. **(a)** Of which type of plate boundary movement is California a good example? [1]

....

(b) Explain what happens at a constructive plate boundary and give an example. [3]

....

....

....

....

....

(c) Explain what happens at a destructive plate boundary and give an example. [3]

....

....

....

....

....

(d) What happens to an oceanic plate when it moves towards a continental plate? [2]

....

....

....

(e) Why do tectonic plates float on the Earth's mantle? Put a tick (✓) in the box next to the correct statement. [1]

Tectonic plates contain helium from meteorite strikes early in the Earth's past. ☐

Tectonic plates are less dense than the mantle and therefore float on top. ☐

Radioactive emissions from the Earth's core bombard the plates and cause them to float. ☐

Tectonic plates are stuck in position and therefore cannot sink. ☐

7. **(a)** Complete the following sentences. Use words from this list. [4]

fusion   gravity   heat   gas   friction

The solar system started as clouds of .... and dust. These clouds were

pulled together by the force of ...., which created intense

.... Nuclear .... began and the Sun was formed.

(b) Draw straight lines from the names of the different masses in the Universe to their correct description. [4]

Mass	Description
Asteroids	Small icy masses that orbit the Sun
Comets	Small rocky masses that orbit the Sun
Dwarf planets	Large masses that orbit the Sun
Moons	Large masses that have not cleared their orbits of other objects
Planets	Rocky masses that orbit planets

(c) Place the following planets in order of the length of time of their orbit. Put the letters in the empty boxes to show the correct order. Start with the shortest. [4]

A Mars **B** Mercury **C** Venus **D** Saturn **E** Jupiter

Shortest ☐ ☐ ☐ ☐ ☐ Longest

8. (a) How old is our Sun? [1]

(b) Explain where the Sun's energy comes from. [2]

(c) Which of the following statements is true? Put a tick (✓) in the box next to the correct statement. [1]

The Universe is approximately 5000 million years old. ☐

The Sun is older than the Universe. ☐

The Universe contains approximately a million galaxies. ☐

The Earth is the same size as the Sun. ☐

Our galaxy contains at least 100 billion stars. ☐

(d) Place the following in order of size. Put the letters in the empty boxes to show the correct order. Start with the smallest. [4]

A The Universe   **B** The Earth   **C** The Sun

D The solar system   **E** A galaxy

Smallest   Largest

(e) Explain what a light-year is and why scientists use them to measure distances in space. [2]

(f) The nearest galaxy to the Milky Way is 2.2 million light-years away. What does this mean about the light we observe from it today? [2]

(g) Name the **two** methods that astronomers can use to work out the distances to different stars. [2]

1.

2.

9. State **three** types of electromagnetic radiation given out by stars. [3]

1.

2.

3.

10. What is light pollution? [1]

11. This question is about the origin of the Universe.

(a) What is the 'Big Bang' theory? [1]

....

....

(b) How many years ago do scientists think the 'Big Bang' happened? [1]

....

12. **(a)** Complete the following sentences. Use words from this list. You may use them more than once. [4]

energy   **light**   **matter**   **sound**   **travels**   **transfers**

All waves transfer .... from one place to another without transferring

.... The .... is transferred in the direction the wave

....

(b) (i) Describe the difference between longitudinal and transverse waves. [2]

....

....

....

....

(ii) Give an example of each type of wave. [2]

Longitudinal: ....

Transverse: ....

(c) (i) Explain what is meant by the **frequency** of a wave. [1]

....

....

(ii) What is the unit for the frequency of a wave? [1]

....

13. Harry and Robert are talking about where the Sun's energy comes from.

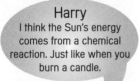

Harry
I think the Sun's energy comes from a chemical reaction. Just like when you burn a candle.

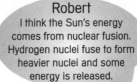

Robert
I think the Sun's energy comes from nuclear fusion. Hydrogen nuclei fuse to form heavier nuclei and some energy is released.

(a) Who is correct, Harry or Robert? [1]

(b) The amount of energy released from the fusion between individual hydrogen nuclei is very small. How could this possibly explain the vast amounts of energy released? [2]

(c) Explain how the life cycle of a star can help to explain where all the elements come from.

🖉 *The quality of written communication will be assessed in your answer to this question.* [6]

[Total: _____ / 86]

14. **(a)** Put a ⟨ring⟩ around the correct options in the following sentences. [2]

P-waves can travel through solids **and / but not** liquids.

S-waves can travel through solids **and / but not** liquids.

(b) Look at the diagram of a cross-section through the Earth.

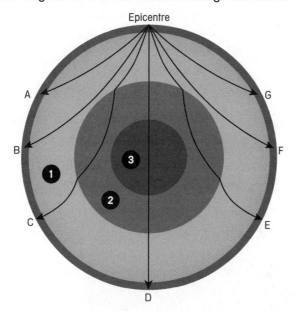

Epicentre

Key:
1 = Mantle (solid)
2 = Outer core (liquid)
3 = Inner core (solid)

(i) At which of the points, **A, B, C, D, E, F** or **G**, will P-waves be detected? [1]

_____

(ii) At which of the points, **A, B, C, D, E, F** or **G**, will S-waves be detected? [1]

_____

(c) Why do waves travel in curved paths through the Earth? [2]

_____

_____

_____

(d) Why are there abrupt changes in the direction of the waves? [2]

_____

_____

_____

15. Explain how the pattern in the magnetisation of seafloor rocks on either side of oceanic ridges can provide evidence for tectonic theory.

✎ *The quality of written communication will be assessed in your answer to this question.* [6]

....

....

....

....

....

....

16. The diagram shows the movement of the tectonic plates.

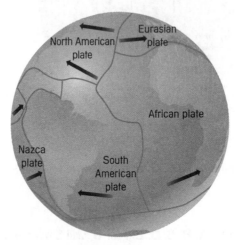

Describe how the movement of the tectonic plates is linked to the rock cycle.

✎ *The quality of written communication will be assessed in your answer to this question.* [6]

....

....

....

....

....

....

17. Light from distant galaxies is red shifted. Use this information to explain why scientists think the Universe is expanding. [2]

....

....

....

18. **(a)** What does the future of the Universe depend on? [1]

....

(b) The Universe may end in a 'big crunch' or it may expand forever. State the conditions necessary for these two different possibilities to occur. [2]

'Big crunch': ....

Expand forever: ....

19. **(a)** Draw straight lines to join the seismic wave to its correct description. [1]

Seismic wave	Description
P-wave	Transverse
S-wave	Longitudinal

(b) The speed of seismic waves in the Earth's crust can be up to 8km/s but in the mantle the speed can be up to 13km/s. Explain why the speed is greater in the mantle. [3]

....

....

....

(c) An earthquake occurs at a depth of 40km within the Earth's crust. If the speed of the P-waves is 6km/s and the speed of the S-waves is 4km/s, calculate the time delay between the two waves reaching the surface. [3]

....

....

.... s

[Total: .... / 32]

1. (a) What are the 'packets' of energy called that a beam of electromagnetic radiation carries? Put a tick (✓) in the box next to the correct answer. [1]

Protons ☐   Electrons ☐

Photons ☐   Neutrons ☐

(b) The electromagnetic spectrum can be arranged in order of wavelength. The regions **A, B, C** and **D** on the diagram are different parts of the electromagnetic spectrum. Write the correct letter in each box. [3]

A   B   C   D

Microwaves ☐   Infrared ☐

X-rays ☐   Gamma rays ☐

2. (a) Name **four** emitters of radiation and a detector that can be used for each one. [4]

Emitter 1: ....   Detector: ....

Emitter 2: ....   Detector: ....

Emitter 3: ....   Detector: ....

Emitter 4: ....   Detector: ....

(b) Materials can absorb, reflect or transmit radiation. Complete the sentences. Use words from this list. [2]

absorbed   **reflected**   **transmitted**

Microwaves are .... when they hit a metal surface.

X-rays are .... by bones.

Visible light is .... by the atmosphere.

3. (a) Give **two** ways in which the intensity of electromagnetic radiation absorbed by an object can be reduced. [2]

....

....

....

....

(b) When photons are absorbed they can produce heat. What does the amount of heat produced depend on? [2]

....

....

4. A group of students is talking about exposure to the Sun.

Anna
My mother had skin cancer but she used to sunbathe a lot.

Tom
I stay indoors between 11am and 3pm when the Sun is at its hottest.

Grace
I go nice and brown in the sun.

Jack
I always use plenty of sun lotion and wear a T-shirt.

Emily
A little ultraviolet is good for you. It gives you vitamin D.

Kieran
I never burn in the sun and am unlikely to suffer any damage from ultraviolet rays.

(a) Which **two** students refer to actions taken to reduce the risks of exposure to ultraviolet radiation? [2]

.... and ....

(b) Which student refers to the dangers of ultraviolet radiation? .... [1]

(c) Which **two** students refer to the benefits of exposure to ultraviolet radiation? [2]

.... and ....

5. Which of the statements about ionising radiation are correct? Put ticks (✓) in the boxes next to the **two** correct statements. [2]

Ionising radiation can break molecules into bits called ions. ☐

X-rays are a type of ionising radiation; gamma rays are not. ☐

Ionising radiation cannot break molecules into bits called ions. ☐

X-rays and gamma rays are types of ionising radiation. ☐

6. **(a)** Which of the following can be used to protect people from the effects of radiation? Put ticks (✓) in the boxes next to the **two** correct statements. [2]

Surrounding nuclear reactors with lead ☐

Wire screens in microwave ovens ☐

Staying in a swimming pool on a hot day ☐

Surrounding nuclear reactors with tin ☐

(b) Why is ionising radiation dangerous to humans? [2]

....

....

....

(c) How do microwaves heat materials? [2]

....

....

7. **(a)** What effect will an increase in the amount of carbon dioxide in the atmosphere have on the Earth? Put a tick (✓) in the box next to the correct answer. [1]

The Earth will cool down. ☐

More radiation will escape. ☐

More heat will be absorbed by the atmosphere. ☐

There will be no effect. ☐

(b) Put a ring around the correct options in the following sentences. [3]

Light radiation from the Sun warms the Earth's surface and is used by plants for

respiration / photosynthesis. This process **increases / decreases** the amount of carbon dioxide

in the atmosphere and **increases / decreases** the amount of oxygen in the atmosphere.

8. (a) Describe the effect that an increase in greenhouse gases has on the heat escaping into space. [1]

....

....

(b) Name the **three** main greenhouse gases. [3]

1. ....

2. ....

3. ....

9. How does the ozone layer help to protect us from radiation from the Sun?

🖋 *The quality of written communication will be assessed in your answer to this question.* [6]

....

....

....

....

....

....

....

10. (a) The diagram shows the carbon cycle. Write the correct letter for each process in the boxes. [3]

Eating of plants ⬜

Photosynthesis ⬜

Respiration ⬜

Death of plants and animals ⬜

(b) Which process removes carbon dioxide from the atmosphere and which organisms take part in this process? [2]

....

....

(c) Explain how the carbon from carbon dioxide in the atmosphere ends up in organisms further up the food chain and is then returned to the atmosphere.

🖉 *The quality of written communication will be assessed in your answer to this question.* [6]

(d) The amount of carbon dioxide in the atmosphere remained constant for thousands of years. Explain how. [2]

(e) Describe the two main processes which have contributed to the increase in carbon dioxide levels in recent times.

🖉 *The quality of written communication will be assessed in your answer to this question.* [6]

11. (a) Although radio signals are not strongly absorbed by the atmosphere, they are not used to transmit signals to satellites. What properties of microwaves make them better suited for transmitting signals to satellites? Put ticks (✓) in the boxes next to the **two** correct statements.   [2]

They have higher energy.   ☐

They are significantly refracted by the atmosphere.   ☐

They have lower energy.   ☐

They are not significantly refracted by the atmosphere. ☐

(b) Name the type of radiation for each of the following uses.   [4]

(i) Taking shadow pictures of bones: ....

(ii) Transmitting radio and TV programmes: ....

(iii) Satellite communication and heating food: ....

(iv) Carrying information along telephone cables: ....

(c) Explain how the properties of X-rays make them suitable for their use(s).   [2]

....

....

....

12. (a) A signal is often added to a high-energy carrier wave so that it can be transmitted long distances. This changes the carrier wave. This is called modulation. Which **two** features of a wave can be affected by modulation? Put ticks (✓) in the boxes next to the **two** correct answers.   [2]

Frequency ☐

Type ☐

Length ☐

Amplitude ☐

(b) What is the role of a receiver in the transmission of information?   [2]

....

....

13. **(a)** What is the main difference between an analogue signal and a digital signal? [1]

....

....

(b) Put a tick (✓) in the correct box to show whether each statement is **true** or **false**. [4]

	true	false
(i) Digital signals can take a range of values between 0 and 1.	☐	☐
(ii) The output of a digitally transmitted signal is of a higher quality than an analogue signal.	☐	☐
(iii) Noise can be easily removed so has little effect on digital signals.	☐	☐
(iv) Digital signals can only take two values: on or off.	☐	☐

(c) (i) On the grid provided, draw the digital signal represented by 1011001. [2]

(ii) On the grid provided, draw an analogue wave with a wavelength of 2cm and an amplitude of 1cm. [2]

(d) When talking about signals we often talk about 'noise'. What do we mean by signal noise? [1]

....

....

(e) Does the diagram show a received digital signal or a received analogue signal? [1]

....

[Total: .... / 83]

14. What **three** factors combine to cause a decrease in the intensity of electromagnetic radiation leaving the Sun's surface and reaching the Earth's atmosphere? [3]

1. ....

2. ....

3. ....

15. Complete the following sentence. [1]

The amount of damage to the skin caused by ultraviolet radiation depends on the intensity of the

radiation and the .... of exposure.

16 Put a ring around the correct options in the following sentence. [2]

Ions are **very reactive / unreactive** and **can / cannot** take part in further chemical reactions.

17. Sunbathing can put you at risk from ultraviolet radiation.

(a) State **two** ways in which you could reduce the risk of exposure to ultraviolet radiation. [2]

1. ....

2. ....

(b) What are the potential dangers of exposure to ultraviolet? [2]

....

....

18. **(a)** Why do climatologists believe that human activity is responsible for global warming? [3]

....

....

....

....

....

(b) Use the carbon cycle to explain how burning forests affects the amount of carbon dioxide in the atmosphere.

🖉 *The quality of written communication will be assessed in your answer to this question.* [6]

....

....

....

....

....

....

....

....

19. **(a)** The diagrams show an analogue signal and a digital signal which have been distorted by noise.

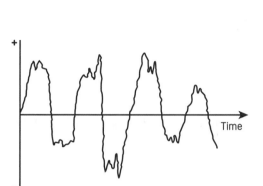

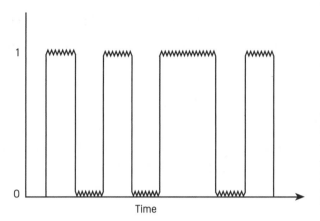

Explain why digital signals can be recovered after the addition of noise and why this is a benefit compared with analogue signals.

🖉 *The quality of written communication will be assessed in your answer to this question.* [6]

_____

_____

_____

_____

_____

_____

_____

_____

(b) Decide whether each statement applies to **analogue signals**, **digital signals** or **both**. [4]

(i) The signal is transmitted as an electromagnetic wave. _____

(ii) The signal is a code made up of 1s and 0s. _____

(iii) The signal is made up of short pulses. _____

(iv) The signal varies in the same way as the original sound wave. _____

[Total: _____ / 29]

1. This question is about alternative power sources.

Charlie makes a model of a hydroelectric power station to show other students the advantages of alternative energy sources. In the model, water is static in a reservoir behind the dam. When water is allowed to flow from the reservoir, it causes a generator to produce electricity, which lights a 12V 36W lamp.

(a) Explain how the generator produces a voltage. [2]

....

....

(b) (i) What energy changes take place in the model to enable the hydroelectric power station to produce electricity? [2]

....

....

(ii) When the generator is running, what is the value of the current flowing through the lamp? [2]

....

.... amps

(iii) If the lamp remains lit for 20 minutes, how much energy, in joules, will the lamp transfer? [2]

....

.... joules

(c) A group of students is talking about alternative energy sources.

Cindy
Using wave power might make the beach unsuitable for surfers.

Alex
I would rather use biofuel as it can be grown easily.

Hakeem
Hydroelectric power doesn't damage the atmosphere but it damages the environment in other ways.

Chloe
I don't think they should build a tidal power station. Trade would suffer.

(i) Which student is concerned about the effect one of the sources might have on tourism? [1]

....

(ii) Which student is talking about a source that could produce greenhouse gases when burned? [1]

....

2. This question is about primary and secondary energy sources.

(a) Which is **not** a primary energy source? Put a tick (✓) in the box next to the correct answer. [1]

Waves ☐   Heat ☐   Electrical ☐   Nuclear ☐   Wind ☐

(b) What do scientists mean when they describe an energy source as a **secondary energy source**? [1]

....

....

3. A new power station needs to be built near to the coast and the final decision will be either coal or nuclear as the primary energy source. The local environmental group is unhappy with both choices and feels that there are better solutions.

(a) Explain **one** problem with using coal and **one** problem with using nuclear power as the primary energy source. [2]

Coal: ....

Nuclear power: ....

(b) Name **two** possible renewable energy sources and explain why the local environmental group might think that these alternative sources are an improvement.

🖉 *The quality of written communication will be assessed in your answer to this question.* [6]

....

....

....

....

....

....

....

....

....

4. The Sankey diagram gives information about the efficiency of energy transfers. Use the diagram to answer the questions below.

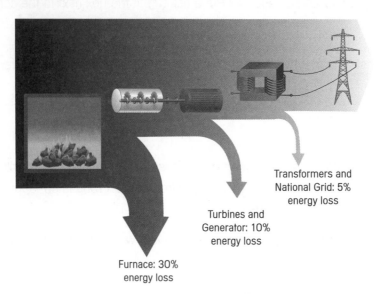

Transformers and National Grid: 5% energy loss

Turbines and Generator: 10% energy loss

Furnace: 30% energy loss

(a) What is the main form in which energy is lost during transfer? [1]

....

(b) How much energy is lost by transformers and the National Grid? [1]

....

(c) What type of fuel could be put in the furnace? [1]

....

(d) For every 100J of energy stored in the coal, how much is reaching the mains supply in homes? Put a ring around the correct answer. [1]

                10J   **30J**   **40J**   **45J**   **55J**

5. In a nuclear power station, uranium is used to produce electricity. Which statement correctly describes the process? Put a tick (✓) in the box next to the correct statement. [1]

Uranium is burned. Heat turns water into steam. Steam turns the generator. ☐

Fuel is burned. Heat turns water into steam. Steam turns a turbine. The turbine drives the generator. ☐

Energy is released from the nucleus. Heat is used to produce steam. Steam turns a turbine. The turbine drives the generator. ☐

Energy is released from the nucleus. Heat is used to turn water into steam. Steam turns the generator. ☐

6. A petrol generator produces an electric current by burning petrol, which is a primary fuel. Which statement below is correct about running a 12V 36W electric drill using the generator? Put a tick (✓) in the box next to the correct statement. [1]

Connecting a large resistance across the output terminals would increase the current to the drill. ☐

Running the generator for longer would increase the current to the drill. ☐

Drawing a larger current from the generator would use up more petrol each second. ☐

Changing the drill for one with a rating of 12V 24W would increase the current to the electric drill. ☐

7. Draw straight lines from each of the alternative energy sources to a question that has to be considered when using them. [2]

Alternative energy source   **Question**

| Wind farm |

| Biofuel |

| Hydroelectric power |

| Is there sufficient farmland available? |

| Is there a suitable place for a dam? |

| Are there any hills to cause turbulence? |

8. The table gives details on ways to save energy.

In the Home	In the Workplace	National Context
Use of more efficient appliances A condensing boiler could save £190 per year	Cleaning air conditioner filters can save 5% of the energy used in running the system	Replace old houses with new efficient ones
Double glazing Possible saving: £130 per year	Using low energy light bulbs	Increased use of public transport
Loft insulation Possible saving: £145 per year	Roof insulation and cavity wall insulation in modern buildings	Use of more efficient trains and buses
Cavity wall insulation Possible saving: £110 per year	Use of efficient, modern, low energy machinery	Encourage more widespread recycling
Draught proof rooms Possible saving: £25 per year	Use of efficient, modern vehicles for transport of goods	Encourage car sharing and fewer journeys

You are a government minister for energy and have to advise on the best ways of saving energy in the home, in the workplace and in a national context.

(a) Name the **two** energy-saving measures in the home that save the most money. [2]

1. ....

2. ....

(b) How much money can be saved in the home over three years by adopting the two best energy-saving measures? [2]

....

....

....

(c) Describe **one** way in which using low energy light bulbs can save money in the workplace. [1]

....

....

(d) In the national context, how can more widespread recycling save energy?

🖉 *The quality of written communication will be assessed in your answer to this question.* [6]

....

....

....

....

....

....

9. The table shows changes to the energy sources used to generate electricity in the UK from 1990–2004.

Energy Source	% Used in 1990	% Used in 2004
Coal	67	33
Gas	0.05	40
Nuclear	18.9	19.2
Renewable sources	0	3.6
Hydroelectric power	1.1	2.6
Oil	6.8	1.1
Other	6.15	0.5

The availability of cheap gas from the North Sea and concerns about pollution and the price of oil have had an effect on the energy sources used in the UK.

Which are **not** true explanations of the data in the table? Put ticks (✓) in the boxes next to the **two incorrect** statements. [2]

Supplies of coal from British mines ran out in the 1990s. ☐

The use of nuclear power remained roughly constant throughout the period. ☐

The use of gas in power stations increased substantially between 1990 and 2004. ☐

The use of hydroelectric power increased after 1990 due to increased rainfall. ☐

Renewable sources were not seriously considered as a main energy source in 1990. ☐

The use of oil in power stations fell due to the rise in price after 1990. ☐

10. This question is about using electricity to power items in the home.

The table gives some information about electrical items and how long they were used for.

Electrical Appliance	Power Rating	Time Used For
Electric heater	4kW	90 minutes
Lamp	100W	8 hours
Electric fire	3000W	30 minutes
Kettle	3000W	2 minutes

The cost of electricity is 8p per unit (kWh).

(a) How much would it cost for the lamp? [2]

....

....

....

(b) If the water inside the kettle receives 1800 joules of energy every second, how efficient is the kettle? [2]

....

....

....

11. Below is a chart showing the production of two primary fuels between 1980 and 2010 in the UK.

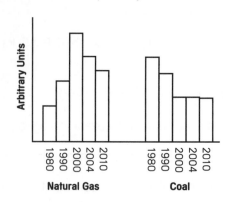

(a) (i) The mass of coal mined fell between 1980 and 2000 but gas production increased during the same period. Suggest why this might have happened. [1]

....

....

(ii) An energy minister said: "No new coal power stations have been built in the UK for the last 10 years." How does the chart support this comment? [1]

....

(b) A student comments that there are limitations to the conclusions that can be made from the data. What is the main limitation that lowers confidence in any conclusion made? [1]

....

....

12. A farmer in Scotland is interested in using her land to generate electricity for the National Grid. She is keen on renewable sources and is unsure whether to choose biofuel, wind or solar as her source for generating electricity. She is advised to use wind turbines by a friend. What reasons might her friend have given for this choice?

✎ *The quality of written communication will be assessed in your answer to this question.* [6]

....

....

....

....

....

....

13. Below are three boxes containing a type of renewable energy source and three boxes containing statements about alternative energy. Draw straight lines to join each source to the correct statement.   [2]

Source	Statement
Solar	Build in exposed areas
Hydroelectric	A dam needs to be built across a river
Wind	It is ideal if the panels face south

14. This question is about how the generation of energy from alternative sources could replace current power stations.

(a) The Government needs to build new power stations to meet the country's energy needs. The choice is between using fossil fuels or nuclear fuel to power them. Give **one** advantage and **one** disadvantage of using any one named fossil fuel and **one** advantage and **one** disadvantage of using nuclear fuel.   [4]

....

....

....

....

(b) (i) People are concerned about building new power stations that burn fossil fuels. Some suggest that only wind farms should be built. Give **two** reasons why this is not a good idea.   [2]

1. ....

....

2. ....

....

(ii) The Government believes that some of our energy requirements could be supplied from wind turbines. It prefers to build new wind farms out at sea. Give **two** advantages and **two** disadvantages of having the wind farms out at sea.   [4]

Advantage 1: ....

Advantage 2: ....

Disadvantage 1: ....

Disadvantage 2: ....

(iii) Wind turbines drive the turbine directly. Give **two** other examples of renewable sources that also drive turbines directly. [2]

1. ....

2. ....

[Total: .... / 68]

15. The table gives information about some of the energy sources used in the United Kingdom.

Energy Source	Problems	Additional Information
Gas	Increase in gas imports as the North Sea supplies fall	Supply and prices controlled by suppliers outside the UK
Coal	Greenhouse gases and particulates Contributes to acid rain	Large stocks underground in the UK
Wind	Expensive to build Variable output	No greenhouse gases Plenty of windy locations in the UK and at sea
Hydroelectric	Need to build dams and flood land Expensive	Limited suitable locations No greenhouse gases
Solar	Needs a large surface area due to low average sunlight intensities in the UK Expensive	Can be used to supplement other energy supplies Can be placed on roofs so unobtrusive
Nuclear	Dealing with radioactive waste	Clean fuel with high energy output Comes from stable regions of the world

Three ministers are discussing the future energy needs of the UK.

Minister A says: "There is only a need for gas. It is cheaper than the others, doesn't produce solid waste and the power stations don't cover as much land as the alternative energy sources do."

Minister B says: "I would only use solar energy or wind power as they are green energy sources and are friendly to the environment."

Minister C says: "You can't just rely on one energy source. There are problems with the alternative energy sources, although they can play their part."

(a) For each of Minister B's choices of energy source, give **one** reason why relying only on them is not a good idea. [2]

Solar energy: ....

....

Wind power: ....

....

(b) Minister A's argument is that the only source of energy needed is gas. Give **one** reason, using the information in the table, why this is not a good idea. [1]

....

....

(c) Minister C mentions that more than one energy source is needed and alternative energy sources can play their part. Explain how alternative energy sources could play their part in providing energy for homes and industry, and why it is important to have more than one energy source.

🖉 *The quality of written communication will be assessed in your answer to this question.* [6]

....

....

....

....

....

....

....

16. This question is about the use of electrical appliances.

Michael is doing some DIY on his home.

(a) He needs to lift a 2000N pallet of bricks 5m from the ground floor to the upstairs balcony. The electric motor takes 25 seconds to do the job. What is the rate at which the motor transfers energy? [2]

....

.... J/s *or* W

(b) Michael uses a 230V electric drill to make a hole in the wall for a lamp fitting. The drill is rated at 1150W.

(i) What current will the drill use from the mains? [2]

....

.... amps

(ii) If the job takes 3 minutes, how much energy, in joules, is transferred? [2]

....

.... joules

(iii) How many units of electricity (kilowatt hours) does the job use? [2]

....

.... kWh

(iv) If the cost of electricity is 8p per kilowatt hour, what will be the cost of the electricity used for the job? [2]

....

.... p

(c) At the end of the day, Michael switches on his washing machine. The efficiency of the motor in the washing machine is 65%. The input power to the motor is 2kW.

(i) What is the useful power output? [2]

....

.... W

(ii) How much useful work will the motor do in 5 minutes? [2]

....

.... joules

[Total: .... / 23]

Periodic Table

Key

relative atomic mass
atomic symbol
name
atomic (proton) number

| 1 | H 1 hydrogen 1 |

Group 1	Group 2											Group 3	Group 4	Group 5	Group 6	Group 7	Group 0
																	4 **He** helium 2
7 **Li** lithium 3	9 **Be** beryllium 4											11 **B** boron 5	12 **C** carbon 6	14 **N** nitrogen 7	16 **O** oxygen 8	19 **F** fluorine 9	20 **Ne** neon 10
23 **Na** sodium 11	24 **Mg** magnesium 12											27 **Al** aluminium 13	28 **Si** silicon 14	31 **P** phosphorus 15	32 **S** sulfur 16	35.5 **Cl** chlorine 17	40 **Ar** argon 18
39 **K** potassium 19	40 **Ca** calcium 20	45 **Sc** scandium 21	48 **Ti** titanium 22	51 **V** vanadium 23	52 **Cr** chromium 24	55 **Mn** manganese 25	56 **Fe** iron 26	59 **Co** cobalt 27	59 **Ni** nickel 28	63.5 **Cu** copper 29	65 **Zn** zinc 30	70 **Ga** gallium 31	73 **Ge** germanium 32	75 **As** arsenic 33	79 **Se** selenium 34	80 **Br** bromine 35	84 **Kr** krypton 36
85 **Rb** rubidium 37	88 **Sr** strontium 38	89 **Y** yttrium 39	91 **Zr** zirconium 40	93 **Nb** niobium 41	96 **Mo** molybdenum 42	[98] **Tc** technetium 43	101 **Ru** ruthenium 44	103 **Rh** rhodium 45	106 **Pd** palladium 46	108 **Ag** silver 47	112 **Cd** cadmium 48	115 **In** indium 49	119 **Sn** tin 50	122 **Sb** antimony 51	128 **Te** tellurium 52	127 **I** iodine 53	131 **Xe** xenon 54
133 **Cs** caesium 55	137 **Ba** barium 56	139 **La*** lanthanum 57	178 **Hf** hafnium 72	181 **Ta** tantalum 73	184 **W** tungsten 74	186 **Re** rhenium 75	190 **Os** osmium 76	192 **Ir** iridium 77	195 **Pt** platinum 78	197 **Au** gold 79	201 **Hg** mercury 80	204 **Tl** thallium 81	207 **Pb** lead 82	209 **Bi** bismuth 83	[209] **Po** polonium 84	[210] **At** astatine 85	[222] **Rn** radon 86
[223] **Fr** francium 87	[226] **Ra** radium 88	[227] **Ac*** actinium 89	[261] **Rf** rutherfordium 104	[262] **Db** dubnium 105	[266] **Sg** seaborgium 106	[264] **Bh** bohrium 107	[277] **Hs** hassium 108	[268] **Mt** meitnerium 109	[271] **Ds** darmstadtium 110	[272] **Rg** roentgenium 111							

Elements with atomic numbers 112–116 have been reported but not fully authenticated

*The lanthanoids (atomic numbers 58–71) and the actinoids (atomic numbers 90–103) have been omitted.
The relative atomic masses of copper and chlorine have not been rounded to the nearest whole number.

Data Sheet

Useful Relationships

The Earth in the Universe

Distance = Wave speed × Time

Wave speed = Frequency × Wavelength

Sustainable Energy

Energy transferred = Power × Time

Power = Voltage × Current

$$\text{Efficiency} = \frac{\text{Energy usefully transferred}}{\text{Total energy supplied}} \times 100\%$$

Notes